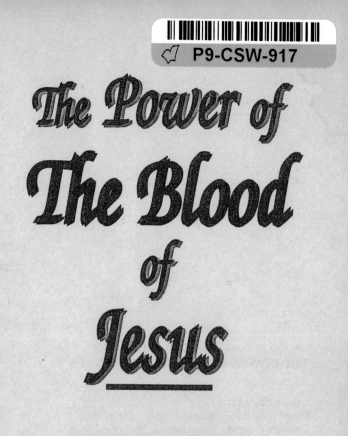

P9-CSW-917

The Power of The Blood of Jesus

ANDREW MURRAY

Whitaker House

THE POWER OF THE BLOOD OF JESUS

ISBN: 0-88368-234-6
Printed in the United States of America
Copyright © 1993 by Whitaker House

Whitaker House
30 Hunt Valley Circle
New Kensington, PA 15068

9 10 11 12 13 14 / 06 05 04 03 02 01 00

Preface

This book is a translation of a portion of a series of addresses by my late father, Rev. Andrew Murray, M.A., D.D., on "The Power of the Blood of Jesus," which hitherto have appeared in Dutch only.

The translator is the Rev. William M. Douglas, B.A., who for many years was my father's intimate friend, having been associated with him in connection with the South African Keswick Convention Movement. During my father's lifetime, he permitted Mr. Douglas to translate his book, *The Prayer Life,* and he became the biographer of my father after his death.

I have read the manuscript and think the translation is excellent. He has reproduced the thoughts of my father exactly.

I feel sure that much blessing will result from the prayerful and thoughtful reading of these chapters.

Trusting you may learn to value and to live in the experience of the power of the precious blood of our Lord and Savior Jesus Christ,

I remain,

Yours in the Blessed Master's service,

M. E. MURRAY

NOTE BY TRANSLATOR: It is necessary to remember that all through these chapters Dr. Murray refers only to "sacrificial blood." The blood in the Bible is always that.

It should be noted when reading Chapter 3 that the Dutch Bible which Dr. Murray used, the word *verzoening* is used for "propitiation." *Verzoening* means "reconciliation" and that is the word used in this translation.

Contents

CHAPTER 1

What the Scriptures Teach about the Blood

"...not without blood..."
—*Hebrews 9:7*

God has spoken to us in the Scriptures in diverse portions and in various manners, but the voice is ever the same. It is always the Word of the same God.

Hence the importance of treating the Bible as a whole and receiving the witness it gives in its various portions concerning certain definite truths. It is thus we learn to recognize the place these truths actually occupy in revelation, or rather in the heart of God. Thus, too, we begin to discover what the foundation truths of the Bible are which, above others, demand attention. Standing as they do, so prominently, in each new departure in God's revelation, remaining unchanged when the dispensation changes, they carry a divine intimation of their importance.

It is my object, in the chapters which follow this introductory one, to show what the Scriptures teach us concerning the glorious power of the blood of Jesus and the wonderful blessings procured for us by it. I cannot lay a better foundation for my exposition, nor give a better proof of the superlative glory of that blood as the power of redemption, than by asking my readers to follow me through the Bible, and thus see the unique place which is given to the blood from the beginning to the end of God's revelation of Himself to man, as recorded in the Bible.

It will become clear that there is no single scriptural idea, from Genesis to Revelation, more constantly and more prominently kept in view, than that expressed by the words, *the blood.* Our inquiry then is what the Scriptures teach us about the blood:

First, in the Old Testament;

Second, in the teaching of our Lord Jesus Himself;

Third, in what the apostles teach;
Fourth, what Saint John tells us of it in Revelation; and

Last, the lessons we can learn from Scripture.

Its record about the blood begins at the gates of Eden. Into the unrevealed mysteries of Eden I do not enter. But in connection with the sacrifice of Abel all is plain. He brought of *"the firstlings of his flock"* to the Lord as a sacrifice, and there, in connection with the first act of worship recorded in the Bible, blood was shed. We learn from Hebrews 11:4 that it was *"by faith"* Abel offered an acceptable sacrifice, and his name stands first in the record of those whom the Bible calls *"believers."* He had this witness borne to him *"that he pleased God."* His faith, and God's good pleasure in him, are closely connected with the sacrificial blood.

In the light of later revelation, this testimony, given at the very beginning of human history, is of deep significance. It shows that there can be no approach to God, no fellowship with Him by faith, no enjoyment of His favor, apart from the blood.

Scripture gives but short notice of the following sixteen centuries. Then came the flood, which was God's judgment on sin, by the destruction of the world of mankind. But God brought forth a new earth from that awful baptism of water.

Notice, however, that the new earth must be baptized also with blood, and the first recorded act of Noah, after he had left the ark, was the offering of a burnt sacrifice to God. As with Abel, so with Noah at a new beginning, it was *"not without blood."*

Sin once again prevailed, and God laid an entirely new foundation for the establishment of His Kingdom on earth.

By the divine call of Abraham, and the miraculous birth of Isaac, God undertook the formation of a people to serve Him. But this purpose was not accomplished apart from the shedding of the blood. This is apparent in the most solemn hour of Abraham's life.

God had already entered into covenant relationship with Abraham, and his faith had already been severely tried, and had stood the test. It was reckoned, or counted to him, for righteousness. Yet he must learn that Isaac, the son of promise, who belonged wholly to God, can be truly surrendered to God only by death. Isaac must die. For Abraham, as well as for Isaac, only by death could freedom from the self-life be obtained.

Abraham must offer Isaac on the altar. That was not an arbitrary command of God. It was the revelation of a divine truth, that it is only through death that a life truly consecrated to God is possible. But it was impossible for Isaac to die and rise again from the dead, for on account of sin, death would hold him fast. But see, his life was spared, and a ram was offered in his place. Through the blood that then flowed on Mount Moriah, his life was spared. He and the people which sprang from him, live before God *"not without blood."* By that blood, however, he was in a figure raised again from the dead. The great lesson of substitution is here clearly taught.

Four hundred years pass, and Isaac has become, in Egypt, the people of Israel. Through her deliverance from Egyptian bondage, Israel was to be recognized as God's first-born among the nations. Here, also, it is *"not without blood."* Neither the electing grace of God, nor His covenant with Abraham, nor the exercise of His omnipotence, which could so easily have destroyed their oppressors, could dispense with the necessity of the blood.

What the blood accomplished on Mount Moriah for one person, who was the father of the nation, must now be experienced by that nation. By the sprinkling of the door frames of the Israelites with the blood of the Paschal lamb; by the institution of the Passover as an enduring ordinance with the words, *"When I see the blood I will pass over you,"* the people were taught that life can be obtained only by the death of a substitute. Life was possible for them only through the blood of a life given in their place, and appropriated by *"the sprinkling of that blood."*

Fifty days later this lesson was enforced in a striking manner. Israel had reached Sinai.

God had given His Law as the foundation of His covenant. That covenant must now be established, but as it is expressly stated in Hebrews 9:7, *"not without blood."* The sacrificial blood must be sprinkled, first on the altar, and then on the book of the covenant, representing God's side of that covenant; then on the people, with the declaration, *"This is the blood of the covenant"* (Exodus 24:8).

It was in that blood the covenant had its foundation and power. It is by the blood alone, that God and man can be brought into covenant fellowship. That which had been foreshadowed at the gate of Eden, on Mount Ararat, on Moriah, and in Egypt, was now confirmed at the foot of Sinai in a most solemn manner. Without blood there could be no access by sinful man to a Holy God.

There is, however, a marked difference between the manner of applying the blood in the former cases as compared with the latter. On Moriah the life was redeemed by the shedding of the blood. In Egypt it was sprinkled on the door posts of the houses; but at Sinai, it was **sprinkled on the persons themselves.** The contact was closer, the application more powerful.

Immediately after the establishment of the covenant, the command was given, *"Let them make me a sanctuary that I may dwell among them"* (Exodus 25:8). They were to enjoy the full blessedness of having the God of the Covenant abiding among them. Through His grace, they may find Him and serve Him in His house.

He Himself gave, with the minutest care, directions for the arrangement and service of that house. But notice that the blood is the center and reason of all this. Draw near to the vestibule of the earthly temple of the Heavenly King, and the first thing visible is the altar of burnt offering, where the sprinkling of blood continues, without ceasing, from morning until evening. Enter the Holy Place, and the most conspicuous thing is the golden altar of incense, which also, together with the veil, is constantly sprinkled with the blood. Ask what lies beyond the Holy Place, and you will be told that it is the Most Holy Place where God dwells. If you ask how He dwells there and how He is approached, you will be told *"not without blood."* The golden throne, where His glory shines, is itself sprinkled with the blood, once every year when the high priest alone enters to bring in the blood and to worship God. The highest act in that worship is the sprinkling of the blood.

If you inquire further, you will be told that always, and for everything, the blood is the one thing needful. At the consecration of the house or of the priests, at the birth of a child, in the deepest penitence on account of sin, in the

13

highest festival—always and in everything—the way to fellowship with God is through the blood alone.

This continued for fifteen hundred years. At Sinai, in the desert, at Shiloh, in the temple on Mount Moriah it continued—till our Lord came to make an end of all shadows by bringing in the substance and by establishing a fellowship with the Holy One, in spirit and truth.

What Our Lord Jesus Himself Teaches about the Blood

With His coming old things passed away, all things became new. He came from the Father in heaven, and can tell us in divine words the way to the Father.

It is sometimes said that the words *"not without blood"* belong to the Old Testament. But what does our Lord Jesus Christ say? Notice, first, that when John the Baptist announced His coming, he spoke of Him as filling a dual office: as *"the Lamb of God that taketh away the sin of the world,"* and then as *"the One who would baptize with the Holy Spirit."* The outpouring of the blood of the Lamb of God must take place, before the outpouring of the Spirit could be bestowed. Only when all that the Old Testament taught about the blood has been fulfilled, can the dispensation of the Spirit begin.

The Lord Jesus Christ Himself plainly declared that His death on the cross was the purpose for which He came into the world: that it was the necessary condition of the redemption and life which He came to bring. He clearly states that in connection with His death, the shedding of His blood was necessary.

In the synagogue at Capernaum He spoke of Himself as *"the Bread of Life"*; of His flesh, *"that He would give it for the life of the world."* Four times over He said most emphatically, *"Except ye...drink his blood ye have no life in you. He that drinketh my blood hath everlasting life. My blood is drink indeed. He that drinketh my blood dwelleth in me and I in him"* (John 6:53-56). Our Lord thus declared the fundamental fact that He Himself, as the Son of the Father, who came to restore to us our lost life, can do this in no other way than by dying for us, by shedding His blood for us, and then making us partakers of its power.

Our Lord confirmed the teaching of the Old Testament offerings—that man can live only through the death of another, and thus obtain a life that through resurrection has become eternal.

But Christ Himself cannot make us partakers of that eternal life which He has procured for us, except by the shedding of His blood, and causing us to drink it. Marvelous fact! *"Not without blood"* can eternal life be ours.

Equally striking is our Lord's declaration of the same truth on the last night of His earthly life. Before He completed the great work of His life by giving it *"as a ransom for many,"* He instituted the Holy Supper, saying, *"This cup is the New Testament in My blood that is shed for you and for many for the remission of sins. Drink ye all of it"* (Matthew 26:28). *"Without shedding of blood there is no remission [of sins]"* (Hebrews 9:22). Without remission of sins there is no life. But by the shedding of His blood He has obtained a new life for us. By what He calls *"the drinking of His blood,"* He shares His life with us. The blood shed in the atonement, which frees us from the guilt of sin and from death—the punishment of sin—the blood, which by faith we drink, bestows on us His life. The blood He shed was, in the first place for us, and is then given to us.

The Teaching of the Apostles under the Inspiration of the Holy Spirit

After His resurrection and ascension, our Lord is not any longer known by the apostles *"after the flesh."* Now, all that was symbolical has passed away, and the deep spiritual truths expressed by symbol, are unveiled.

16

But there is no veiling of the blood. It still occupies a prominent place.

Turn first to the epistle to the Hebrews, which was written purposely to show that the temple service had become unprofitable, and was intended by God to pass away, now that Christ had come.

Here, if anywhere, it might be expected that the Holy Spirit would emphasize the true spirituality of God's purpose, yet it is just here that the blood of Jesus is spoken of in a manner that imparts a new value to the phrase.

We read concerning our Lord that *"by His own blood he entered in the holy place"* (Hebrews 9:12). *"The blood of Christ shall purge your conscience"* (Hebrews 9:14). *"Having therefore, brethren, boldness to enter into the holiest by the blood of Jesus"* (Hebrews 10:19). *"Ye are come to Jesus the Mediator of the New Covenant, and to the blood of sprinkling"* (Hebrews 12:24). *"Jesus also, that he might sanctify the people with his own blood suffered without the gate"* (Hebrews 13:12-13). *"God brought again from the dead our Lord Jesus through the blood of the everlasting covenant"* (Hebrews 13:20).

By such words the Holy Spirit teaches us that the blood is really the central power of our entire redemption. *"Not without blood"* is as valid in the New Testament as in the Old.

Nothing but the blood of Jesus, shed in His death for sin, can cover sin on God's side or remove it on ours.

We find the same teaching in the writings of the apostles. Paul writes of *"being justified freely by his grace through the redemption that is in Christ Jesus...through faith in his blood"* (Romans 3:24, 25); of *"being now justified by his blood"* (Romans 5:9).

To the Corinthians he declares that the *"cup of blessing which we bless is the communion of the blood of Christ"* (1 Corinthians 10:16).

In the epistle to the Galatians he uses the word *cross* to convey the same meaning, while in Colossians he unites the two words and speaks of *"the blood of his cross"* (Galatians 6:14; Colossians 1:20).

He reminds the Ephesians that *"we have redemption through his blood,"* and that we *"are made nigh by the blood of Christ"* (Ephesians 1:7, 2:13).

Peter reminds his readers that they were *"Elect...unto obedience and sprinkling of the blood of Jesus"* (1 Peter 1:2), that they were redeemed by *"the precious blood of Christ"* (1 Peter 1:19).

See how John assures his *"little children"* that *"the blood of Jesus Christ his Son cleanseth us from all sin"* (1 John 1:7). The Son is He *"who came not by water only but by water and blood"* (1 John 1:6).

All of them agree together in mentioning the blood and in glorying in it, as the power by which eternal redemption through Christ is fully accomplished and is then applied by the Holy Spirit.

But perhaps this is merely earthly language. What has heaven to say?

What the Book of Revelation Says Concerning the Blood

It is of the greatest importance to notice, that in the revelation which God has given in this book, of the glory of His throne, and the blessedness of those who surround it, the blood still retains its remarkably prominent place.

On the throne John saw *"a Lamb as it had been slain"* (Revelation 5:6). As the elders fell down before the Lamb, they sang a new song saying, *"Thou art worthy...for thou wast slain and hast redeemed us to God by thy blood"* (Revelation 5:8-9).

Later on when he saw the great company which no man could number, he was told in reply to his question as to who they were, *"They have washed their robes, and made them white in the blood of the Lamb."*

Then again, when he heard the song of victory over the defeat of Satan, its strain was,

"They overcame him by the blood of the Lamb" (Revelation 12:11).

In the glory of heaven, as seen by John, there was no phrase by which the great purposes of God, the wondrous love of the Son of God, the power of His redemption, and the joy and thanksgiving of the redeemed could be gathered up and expressed save this: *"the blood of the Lamb."*

Lessons to Learn from the Scriptures

From the beginning to the end of Scripture, from the closing of the gates of Eden to the opening of the gates of the heavenly Zion, there runs through Scripture a golden thread. It is the blood that unites the beginning and the end, that gloriously restores what sin had destroyed.

It is not difficult to see what lessons the Lord wishes us to learn from the fact that the blood occupies such a prominent place in Scripture.

The Only Means of Dealing with Sin

God has no other way of dealing with sin, or the sinner, save through the blood. For victory over sin and the deliverance of the sinner, God has no other means or thought than *"the blood of Christ."* Yes, it is indeed something that surpasses all understanding.

All the wonders of grace are focused here: the incarnation, by which He took upon Himself our flesh and blood; the love, that spared not itself but surrendered itself to death; the righteousness, which could not forgive sin till the penalty was borne; the substitution, by which He the Righteous One atoned for us, the unrighteous; the atonement for sin, and the justification of the sinner. Thus made possible renewed fellowship with God, together with the cleansing and sanctification to fit us for the enjoyment of that fellowship; the true oneness in life with the Lord Jesus, as He gives us His blood to drink; the eternal joy of the hymn of praise, *"Thou hast redeemed us to God."* All these are but rays of the wondrous light which are reflected upon us from *"the precious blood of Jesus."*

The Right View of the Blood

The blood must have the same place in our hearts which it has with God. From the beginning of God's dealings with man, yes, from before the foundation of the world, the heart of God has rejoiced in that blood. Our heart will never rest, nor find salvation, till we too learn to walk and glory in the power of that blood.

It is not only the penitent sinner, longing for pardon, who must thus value it. No! The redeemed will experience that just as God in His temple sits upon a throne of grace, where the blood is ever in evidence, so there is nothing that draws our hearts nearer to God, filling them with God's love, and joy, and glory, as living in constant, spiritual view of that blood.

The Blessing and Power of the Blood

Let us take time and trouble to learn the full blessing and power of that blood. The blood of Jesus is the greatest mystery of eternity, the deepest mystery of the divine wisdom. Let us not imagine that we can easily grasp its meaning. God thought 4,000 years necessary to prepare men for it, and we also must take time, if we are to gain a knowledge of the power of the blood.

Even taking time is of no avail, unless there is definite taking of sacrificial trouble. Sacrificial blood always meant the offering of a life. The Israelite could not obtain blood for the pardon of his sin, unless the life of something that belonged to him was offered in sacrifice. The Lord Jesus did not offer up His own life, and shed His blood to spare us from the sacrifice of our lives. No, indeed! Rather He did so to make the sacrifice of our lives possible and desirable.

The hidden value of His blood is the spirit of self-sacrifice, and where the blood really touches the heart, it works out in that heart a like spirit of self-sacrifice. We learn to give up ourselves and our lives, so as to press into the full power of that new life, which the blood has provided.

We give our time in order that we may become acquainted with these things by God's Word. We separate ourselves from sin and worldly-mindedness and self-will, that the power of the blood may not be hindered, for it is just these things that the blood seeks to remove.

We surrender ourselves wholly to God in prayer and faith, so as not to think our own thoughts, and not to hold our own lives as a prize, but as possessing nothing save what He bestows. Then He reveals to us the glorious and blessed life which has been prepared for us by the blood.

The Revelation of the Power of the Blood

We can rely upon the Lord Jesus to reveal to us the power of His blood. It is by this confident trust in Him that the blessing obtained by the blood becomes ours. We must never, in thought, separate the blood from the High Priest who shed it, and ever lives to apply it.

He who once gave His blood for us, will, oh so surely, every moment, impart its efficacy. Trust Him to do this. Trust Him to open your eyes, and to give you a deeper spiritual insight. Trust Him to teach you to think about the blood as God thinks about it. Trust Him to impart to you, and to make effective in you, all that He enables you to see.

Trust Him above all, in the power of His eternal High Priesthood, to work out in you, unceasingly, the full merits of His blood, so that your whole life may be an uninterrupted abiding in the sanctuary of God's presence.

Believer, you who have come to the knowledge of the precious blood, hearken to the invitation of your Lord. Come nearer. Let Him teach you; let Him bless you. Let Him cause His blood to become to you spirit, and life, and power, and truth.

Begin now, at once, to open your soul in faith, to receive the full, mighty, heavenly effects of the precious blood, in a more glorious manner than you have ever experienced. He Himself will work these things out in your life.

CHAPTER 2

Redemption by Blood

"Ye know that ye were not redeemed with corruptible things...but with the precious blood of Christ as of a lamb without blemish and without spot."
—1 Peter 1:18-19

The shedding of His blood was the culmination of the sufferings of our Lord. The atoning efficacy of those sufferings was in that shed blood. It is therefore of great importance that the believer should not rest satisfied with the mere acceptance of the blessed truth that he is redeemed by that blood, but should press on to a fuller knowledge of what is meant by that statement and to learn what that blood is intended to do in a surrendered soul.

Its effects are manifold, for we read in Scripture of:

Reconciliation through the blood;
Cleansing through the blood;
Sanctification through the blood;

Union with God through the blood;
Victory over Satan through the blood;
Life through the blood.

These are separate blessings but are all included in one phrase: redemption by the blood. It is only where the believer understands what these blessings are, and by what means they may become his, that he can experience the full power of redemption.

Before passing on to consider in detail these several blessings, let us first inquire, in a more general way, concerning the power of the blood of Jesus:

First, wherein does the power of that blood lie?

Second, what has that power accomplished?

Third, how can we experience its effects?

Wherein Does the Power of That Blood Lie?

What is it that gives to the blood of Jesus such power? How is it that, in the blood alone, there is power possessed by nothing else?

The answer to this question is found in Leviticus 17:11 and 14, *"The life of the flesh is in the blood,"* and *"I have given it to you upon the altar to make an atonement for your souls, for it is the blood that maketh an atonement for the soul."*

It is because the soul, or life, is in the blood and that the blood is offered to God on the altar, that it has in it redemptive power.

The Life Is in the Blood

The value of the blood corresponds to the value of the life that is in it. The life of a sheep or goat is of less value than the life of an ox, and so the blood of a sheep or a goat in an offering is of less value than the blood of an ox (Leviticus 4:3, 14, 27). The life of man is more valuable than that of many sheep or oxen.

And now who can tell the value or the power of the blood of Jesus? In that blood, dwelt the soul of the holy Son of God. The eternal life of the Godhead was carried in that blood (Acts 20:28).

The power of that blood in its many effects is nothing less than the eternal power of God Himself. What a glorious thought for everyone who desires to experience the full power of the blood!

Offered to God on the Altar

But the power of the blood lies above everything else in the fact that it is offered to God on the altar for redemption. When we think of blood as shed, we think of death; death follows when the blood or the soul is poured out. Death makes us think of sin, for death is the punishment of sin. God gave Israel the blood on the altar, as the atonement or covering for sin; that means the sins of the transgressor were laid on the victim, and its death was reckoned as the death or punishment for the sins laid upon it.

The blood was thus the life given up to death for the satisfaction of the law of God, and in obedience to His command. Sin was so entirely covered and atoned for, it was no longer reckoned as that of the transgressor. He was forgiven.

But all these sacrifices and offerings were only types and shadows, till the Lord Jesus came. His blood was the reality to which these types pointed.

His blood was in itself of infinite value, because it carried His soul or life. But the atoning virtue of His blood was infinite also, because of the manner in which it was shed. In holy obedience to the Father's will, He subjected Himself to the penalty of the broken law by pouring out His soul unto death. By that death, not only was the penalty borne, but the law was satisfied, and the Father glorified. His blood atoned for sin, and thus made it powerless. It has a marvelous power for removing sin and opening heaven for the sinner, whom it cleanses and sanctifies and makes meet for heaven.

It is because of the Wonderful Person whose blood was shed, and because of the wonderful way in which it was shed, fulfilling the law of God while satisfying its just demands, that the blood of Jesus has such wonderful power. It is the blood of atonement, and hence it has such efficacy to redeem, accomplishing everything for and in the sinner that is necessary to salvation.

What Has That Power Accomplished?

As we see something of the wonders that power has accomplished, we shall be encouraged to believe that it can do the same for us. Our best plan is to note how the Scriptures glory in the great things which have taken place through the power of the blood of Jesus.

The Blood Opened the Grave

We read in Hebrews 13:20, *"Now the God of peace that brought again from the dead our*

Lord Jesus, that great Shepherd of the sheep, through the blood of the everlasting covenant." It was through the virtue of the blood that God raised up Jesus from the dead. God's almighty power was not exerted to raise Jesus from the dead, apart from the blood.

He came to earth as surety and bearer of the sin of mankind. It was through the shedding of His blood alone that He had the right, as man, to rise again and to obtain eternal life through resurrection. His blood had satisfied the law and righteousness of God. By so doing, He had overcome the power of sin and brought it to naught. So, also, death was defeated, as its sting, sin, had been removed; and the devil also was defeated, who had the power of death, having now lost all right over Him and us. His blood had destroyed the power of death, the devil and hell: the blood of Jesus has opened the grave.

He who truly believes that, perceives the close connection which exists between the blood and the almighty power of God. It is only through the blood that God exerts His almightiness in dealing with sinful men. Where the blood is, there the resurrection power of God gives entrance into eternal life. The blood has made a complete end of all the power of death and hell. Its effects surpass all human thought.

The Blood of Jesus Opened Heaven

We read in Hebrews 9:12, Christ *"by His own blood entered in once for all into the holy place, having obtained eternal redemption for us."*

We know that in the Old Testament tabernacle God's manifested presence was inside the veil. No power of man could remove that veil. The high priest alone could enter there, but only with blood, or the loss of his own life. That was a picture of the power of sin in the flesh, which separates us from God. The eternal righteousness of God guarded the entrance to the Most Holy Place, that no flesh might approach Him.

But now our Lord appears, not in a material but in the true Temple. As High Priest and representative of His people, He asks for Himself, and for sinful children of Adam, an entrance into the presence of the Holy One. *"That where I am, there they may be also"* is His request. He asks that heaven may be opened for each one, even for the greatest sinner, who believes in Him. His request is granted. But how is that? It is through the blood. He entered through His own blood. The blood of Jesus has opened heaven.

So it is ever and always through the blood that the throne of grace remains settled in heaven. In the midst of the seven great realities of heaven (Hebrews 12:22, 24), yes, nearest to God, the Judge of all, and to Jesus the Mediator, the Holy Spirit gives a prominent place to *"the blood of sprinkling."*

It is the constant "speaking" of that blood that keeps heaven open for sinners and sends streams of blessing down on earth. It is through that blood that Jesus, as Mediator, carries on without ceasing His mediatorial work. The throne of grace owes its existence ever and always to the power of that blood.

Oh, the wonderful power of the blood of Christ. Just as it has broken open the gates of the grave, and of hell, to let Jesus out, and us with Him; so it has opened the gates of heaven for Him, and us with Him, to enter. The blood has an almighty power over the kingdom of darkness and hell beneath, and over the kingdom of heaven and its glory above.

All Powerful in the Human Heart

Since it avails so powerfully with God and over Satan, does it not avail even more powerfully with man, for whose sake it was actually shed? We may be sure of it.

The wonderful power of the blood is especially manifested on behalf of sinners on earth. Our text is but one out of many places in Scripture where this is emphasized. *"Ye were redeemed...from your vain conversation with the precious blood of Christ*" (1 Peter 1:18-19).

The word redeemed has a depth of meaning. It indicates particularly deliverance from slavery by emancipation or purchase. The sinner is enslaved under the hostile power of Satan, the curse of the Law, and sin. Now it is proclaimed *"ye are redeemed through the blood,"* which had paid the debt of guilt and destroyed the power of Satan, the curse, and sin.

Where this proclamation is heard and received, there redemption begins in a true deliverance from a vain manner of life, from a life of sin. The word *redemption* includes everything God does for a sinner from the pardon of sin, in which it begins (Ephesians 1:14, 4:30), to the full deliverances of the body by resurrection (Romans 3:23-24).

Those to whom Peter wrote (1 Peter 1:2) were *"elect...to the sprinkling of the blood of Jesus Christ."* It was the proclamation about the precious blood that had touched their hearts and brought them to repentance, awakening faith in them, and filling their souls with life and joy. Each believer was an illustration of the wonderful power of the blood.

Further on, when Peter exhorts them to holiness, it is still the precious blood which is his plea. On that he would fix their eyes.

For the Jew in his self-righteousness and hatred of Christ, for the heathen in his godlessness, there was only one means of deliverance from the power of sin. It is still the one power that effects daily deliverance for sinners. How could it be otherwise? The blood that availed so powerfully in heaven and over hell, is all-powerful also in a sinner's heart. It is impossible for us to think too highly, or to expect too much, from the power of Jesus' blood.

How Does This Power Work?

This is our third question. In what conditions, under what circumstances, can that power secure, unhindered in us, the mighty results it is intended to produce?

The Power Works through Faith

The first answer is that, just as it is everywhere in the kingdom of God, it is through faith. But faith is largely dependent on knowledge. If knowledge of what the blood can accomplish is imperfect, faith expects little, and the more powerful effects of the blood are impossible. Many Christians think that if now, through faith in the blood, they have received the assurance of the pardon of their sins, they have a sufficient knowledge of its effects.

They have no idea that the words of God, like God Himself, are inexhaustible, that they have a wealth of meaning and blessing that surpasses all understanding.

They do not remember that when the Holy Spirit speaks of cleansing through the blood, such words are only the imperfect human expressions of the effects and experiences by which the blood, in an unspeakably glorious manner, will reveal its heavenly life-giving power to the soul. Feeble conceptions of its power prevent the deeper, and more perfect manifestations of its effects.

As we seek to find out what the Scripture teaches about the blood, we shall see that faith in the blood, even as we now understand it, can produce in us greater results than we have yet known; and in future, a ceaseless blessing may be ours.

Our faith may be strengthened by noticing what the blood has already accomplished. Heaven and hell bear witness to that. Faith will grow by exercising confidence in the fathomless fullness of the promises of God. Let us heartily expect that as we enter more deeply into the fountain, its cleansing, quickening, life-giving power will be revealed more blessedly.

We know that in bathing we enter into the most intimate relationship with the water, giving ourselves up to its cleansing effects. The blood of Jesus is described as a *"fountain opened for sin and uncleanness"* (Zechariah 12:1). By the power of the Holy Spirit, it streams through the heavenly temple. By faith, I place myself in closest touch with this heavenly stream; I yield myself to it; I let it cover me and go through me. I bathe in the fountain. It cannot withhold its cleansing and strengthening power. I must in simple faith turn away from what is seen, to plunge into that spiritual fountain, which represents the Savior's blood, with the assurance that it will manifest its blessed power in me.

So let us with childlike, persevering, expectant faith, open our souls to an ever increasing experience of the wonderful power of the blood.

The Spirit and the Blood

But there is still another reply to the question as to what else is necessary, that the blood may manifest its power. Scripture connects the blood most closely with the Spirit. It is only where the Spirit works that the power of the blood will be manifested.

We read in First John that *"there are three that bear witness on earth, the Spirit, and the water and the blood: and these three are one"* (1 John 5:8). The water refers to baptism unto repentance and the laying aside of sin. The blood witnesses to redemption in Christ. The Spirit is He who supplies power to the water and the blood. So also the Spirit and the blood are associated in Hebrews 9:14, where we read, *"How much more shall the blood of Christ, who through the eternal Spirit offered himself without spot to God, purge your conscience."* It was by the eternal Spirit in our Lord, that His blood had its value and power. It is always through the Spirit that the blood possesses its living dowery in heaven and in the hearts of men.

The blood and the Spirit ever bear testimony together. Where the blood is honored in faith or preaching, there the Spirit works; and where He works, He always leads souls to the blood. The Holy Spirit could not be given till the blood was shed. The living bond between the Spirit and the blood cannot be broken.

It should be seriously noticed that, if the full power of the blood is to be manifested in our souls, we must place ourselves under the teaching of the Holy Spirit.

We must firmly believe that He is in us, carrying on His work in our hearts. We must live as those who know that the Spirit of God really dwells within, as a seed of life, and He will bring to perfection the hidden, powerful effects of the blood. We must allow Him to lead us.

Through the Spirit, the blood will cleanse, sanctify, and unite us to God. When the apostle desired to arouse believers to hearken to God's voice with His call to holiness, *"Be ye holy, for I am holy,"* he reminded them that they had been redeemed by the precious blood of Christ.

Knowledge Is Necessary

They must know that they have been redeemed and what that redemption signified, but they must above all know that *"it was not by corruptible things such as silver and gold,"* things in which there was no power of life, *"but by the precious blood of Christ."* To have a correct perception of what the preciousness of that blood was (as the power of a perfect redemption), would be to them the power of a new and holy life.

Beloved Christians, that statement concerns us also. We must know that we are redeemed by the precious blood. We must know about redemption and the blood before we can experience its power.

In proportion as we more fully understand what redemption is, and what the power and preciousness of the blood are, by which redemption has been obtained, we shall the more fully experience its value.

Need and Desire

Let us take ourselves to the school of the Holy Spirit to be led into a deeper knowledge of redemption through the precious blood. Two things are needful for this: first, a deeper sense of need; and second, a desire to understand the blood better. The blood has been shed to take away sin. The power of the blood is to bring to naught the power of sin.

We are, alas, too easily satisfied with the first beginnings of deliverance from sin. Oh, that what remains of sin in us might become unbearable to us! May we no longer be contented with the fact that we, as redeemed ones, sin against God's will in so many things.

May the desire for holiness become stronger in us. Should not the thought that the blood has more power than we know of, and can do for us greater things than we have yet experienced, cause our hearts to go out in strong desire? If there were more desire for deliverance from sin, for holiness and intimate friendship with a Holy God, it would be the first thing that is needful for being led further into the knowledge of what the blood can do.

Expectation

The second thing will follow. Desire must become expectation.

As we inquire from the Word, in faith, what the blood has accomplished, it must be a settled matter with us that the blood can manifest its full power also in us. No sense of unworthiness, or of ignorance, or of helplessness must cause us to doubt. The blood works in the surrendered soul with a ceaseless power of life.

Surrender yourself to God the Holy Spirit.

Fix the eyes of your heart on the blood.

Open your whole inner being to its power.

Shelter under the ever-continuing sprinkling of the blood. The blood on which the throne of grace in heaven is founded, can make your heart the temple and throne of God.

Ask the Lamb of God Himself to make the blood efficacious in you.

You will surely experience that there is nothing to compare with the wonder-working power of the blood of Jesus.

CHAPTER 3

Reconciliation Through the Blood

"Being justified freely by his grace through the
redemption *that is in Christ Jesus, whom
God hath set forth as a propitiation
[reconciliation] though faith in His blood"*
—Romans 3:24-25

As we have seen, several distinct blessings
have been procured for us by the power of the
blood of Jesus, which are all included in the
one word *redemption*. Among these blessings,
reconciliation takes the first place. *"God hath
set forth Jesus as a reconciliation through faith
in his blood."* In our Lord's work of redemption,
reconciliation naturally comes first. It stands
first also among the things the sinner has to
do, who desires to have a share in redemption.
Through it, a participation in the other blessings of redemption is made possible.

Of great importance also is that the believer, who has already received reconciliation, should obtain a deeper and more spiritual conception of its meaning and blessedness. If the power of the blood in redemption is rooted in reconciliation, then a fuller knowledge of what reconciliation is, is the surest way to obtain a fuller experience of the power of the blood. The heart that is surrendered to the teaching of the Holy Spirit will surely learn what reconciliation means. May our hearts be opened wide to receive it.

To understand what reconciliation by the blood means let us consider:

First, sin which has made reconciliation necessary;

Second, God's holiness which fore-ordained it;

Third, the blood of Jesus which obtained it; and

Last, the pardon which results from it.

Sin Made Reconciliation Necessary

In all the work of Christ, and above all in reconciliation, God's object is the removal and destruction of sin. Knowledge of sin is necessary for the knowledge of reconciliation.

We want to understand what there is in sin that needs reconciliation, and how reconciliation renders sin powerless. Then faith will have something to take hold of, and the experience of that blessing is made possible.

Sin has had a twofold effect. It has had an effect on God, as well as on man. We emphasize generally its effect on man. But the effect it has exercised on God is more terrible and serious. It is because of its effect on God that sin has its power over us. God, as Lord of all, could not overlook sin. It is His unalterable law that sin must bring forth sorrow and death. When man fell into sin, he, by that law of God, was brought under the power of sin. So it is with the law of God that redemption must begin, for if sin is powerless against God, and the law of God gives sin no authority over us, then its power over us is destroyed. The knowledge that sin is speechless before God assures us that it has no longer authority over us.

What then was the effect of sin upon God? In His divine nature, He ever remains unchanged and unchangeable, but in His relationship and bearing towards man, an entire change has taken place. Sin is disobedience, a contempt of the authority of God; it seeks to rob God of His honor, as God and Lord. Sin is determined opposition to a holy God. It not only can, but must awaken His wrath.

While it was God's desire to continue in love and friendship with man, sin has compelled Him to become an opponent. Although the love of God towards man remains unchanged, sin made it impossible for Him to admit man into fellowship with Himself. It has compelled Him to pour out upon man His wrath and curse and punishment, instead of His love. The change which sin has caused in God's relationship to man is awful.

Man is guilty before God. Guilt is debt. We know what debt is. It is something that one person can demand from another, a claim which must be met and settled.

When sin is committed, its after-effects may not be noticed, but its guilt remains. The sinner is guilty. God cannot disregard His own demand that sin must be punished; and His glory, which has been dishonored, must be upheld. As long as the debt is not discharged, or the guilt expiated, it is, in the nature of the case, impossible for a holy God to allow the sinner to come into His presence.

We often think that the great question for us is how we can be delivered from the indwelling power of sin, but that is a question of less importance than how we can be delivered from the guilt which is heaped up before God. Can the guilt of sin be removed? Can the effect of sin upon God, in awakening His wrath, be removed? Can sin be blotted out before God? If these things can be done, the power of sin will be broken in us also. Tthe guilt of sin can be removed only through reconciliation.

The word translated "reconciliation" means actually "to cover." Even heathen people had an idea of this. But in Israel, God revealed a reconciliation which could so truly cover and remove the guilt of sin that the original relationship between God and man can be entirely restored. This is what true reconciliation must do. It must so remove the guilt of sin, that is the effect of sin on God, that man can draw near to God in the blessed assurance that there is not any longer the least guilt resting on him to keep him away from God.

Reconciliation Foreordained by the Holiness of God

This must also be considered if we are to understand reconciliation aright. God's holiness is His infinite, glorious perfection, which leads Him always to desire what is good in others as well as in Himself. He bestows, and works out what is good in others, and hates and condemns all that is opposed to what is good.

In His holiness both the love and wrath of God are united: His love which bestows itself; His wrath which, according to the divine law of righteousness, casts out and consumes what is evil. It is as the Holy One that God ordained reconciliation in Israel, and took up His abode on the Mercy Seat. It is as the Holy One that He, in expectation of New Testament times, said so often, *"I am thy Redeemer, the Holy One of Israel."* It is as the Holy One that God wrought out His counsel of reconciliation in Christ.

The wonder of this counsel is that both the holy love and the holy wrath of God find satisfaction in it. Apparently they were in irreconcilable strife with one another. The holy love was unwilling to let man go. Notwithstanding all his sin, it could not give him up. He must be redeemed. The holy wrath could not surrender its demands. The law had been despised. God had been dishonored. God's right must be upheld. There could be no thought of releasing the sinner as long as the law was not satisfied. The terrible effect of sin in heaven on God must be counteracted; the guilt of sin must be removed; otherwise the sinner could not be delivered. The only solution possible was reconciliation.

We have seen that reconciliation means covering. It means that something else has taken the place where sin was established, so that sin can no longer be seen by God.

But because God is the Holy One, and His eyes as a flame of fire, that which covered sin must be something of such a nature that it really counteracted the evil that sin had done, and also that it so blotted out sin before God that it was really destroyed and was not now to be seen.

Reconciliation for sin can take place only by satisfaction. Satisfaction is reconciliation. And as satisfaction is through a substitute, sin can be punished, and the sinner saved. God's holiness also would be glorified and its demands would be met, as well as the demand of God's love in the redemption of the sinner and the demand of His righteousness in the maintenance of the glory of God and of His law.

We know how this was set forth in the Old Testament laws of the offerings. A clean beast took the place of a guilty man. His sin was laid, by confession, on the head of the victim, which bore the punishment by surrendering its life unto death. Then the blood, representing a clean life that now through the bearing of punishment is free from guilt, can be brought into God's presence; the blood or life of the beast that has borne the punishment in place of the sinner. That blood made reconciliation, and covered the sinner and his sin, because it had taken his place and atoned for his sin.

There was reconciliation in the blood. But that was not a reality. The blood of cattle or of goats could never take away sin; it was only a shadow, a picture, of the real reconciliation.

Blood of a totally different character was necessary for an effectual covering of guilt. According to the counsel of the Holy God, nothing less than the blood of God's own Son could bring about reconciliation. Righteousness demanded it; Love offered it. *"Being justified freely by his grace through the redemption that is in Christ Jesus whom God hath set forth for a reconciliation through faith in his blood"* (Romans 3:24-25).

Reconciliation Obtained by the Blood of Jesus

Reconciliation must be the satisfaction of the demands of God's holy law. The Lord Jesus accomplished that. By a willing and perfect obedience, He fulfilled the law under which He had placed Himself. In the same spirit of complete surrender to the will of the Father, He bore the curse which the law had pronounced against sin. He rendered, in fullest measure of obedience or punishment, all that the law of God could ever ask or desire. The law was perfectly satisfied by Him. But how can His fulfilling of the demands of the law be reconciliation for the sins of others? Because, both in creation and in the holy covenant of grace that the Father had made with Him, He was recognized as the head of the human race.

Because of this, He was able, by becoming flesh, to become a second Adam. When He, the Word, became flesh, He placed Himself in a real fellowship with our flesh which was under the power of sin, and He assumed the responsibility for all that sin had done in the flesh against God. His obedience and perfection was not merely that of one man among others, but that of Him who had placed Himself in fellowship with all other men, and who had taken their sin upon Himself.

As head of mankind through creation, as their representative in the covenant, He became their surety. As a perfect satisfaction of the demands of the law was accomplished by the shedding of His blood, this was the reconciliation; the covering of our sin.

Above all, we must never forget that He was God. This bestowed a divine power on Him, to unite Himself with His creatures, and to take them up into Himself. It bestowed on His sufferings a virtue of infinite holiness and power. It made the merit of His blood-shedding more than sufficient to deal with all the guilt of human sin. It made His blood such a real reconciliation, such a perfect covering of sin, that the holiness of God no longer beholds it. It has been, in truth, blotted out. The blood of Jesus, God's Son, has procured a real, perfect and eternal reconciliation.

What does that mean?

We have spoken of the awful effect of sin on God, of the terrible change which took place in heaven through sin. Instead of favor, and friendship, and blessing, and the life of God from Heaven, man had nothing to look for except wrath, curse, death, and perdition. He could think of God only with fear and terror, without hope, and without love. Sin never ceased to call for vengeance; guilt must be dealt with in full.

But see! The blood of Jesus, God's Son, has been shed. Atonement for sin has been made. Peace is restored. A change has taken place again, as real and widespread as that which sin had brought about. For those who receive the reconciliation, sin has been brought to naught. The wrath of God turns round and hides itself in the depth of divine love.

The righteousness of God no longer terrifies man. It meets him as a friend, with an offer of complete justification. God's countenance beams with pleasure and approval as the penitent sinner draws near to Him, and He invites him to intimate fellowship. He opens for him treasure of blessing. There is nothing now that can separate him from God.

The reconciliation through the blood of Jesus has covered his sins; they appear no longer in God's sight. He no longer imputes sin. Reconciliation has wrought out a perfect and eternal redemption.

Oh, who can tell the worth of that precious blood?

It is no wonder that forever mention will be made of that blood in the song of the redeemed, and through all eternity. As long as heaven lasts, the praise of the blood will resound. *"Thou wast slain and hast redeemed us unto God by thy blood."*

But here is the wonder, that the redeemed on earth do not more heartily join in that song, and that they are not abounding in praise for the reconciliation that the power of the blood has accomplished.

Pardon Follows Reconciliation

That the blood has made reconciliation for sin and covered it, and that as a result of this, such a wonderful change has taken place in the heavenly realms—all this will avail us nothing, unless we obtain a personal share in it.

It is in the pardon of sin this takes place. God has offered a perfect acquittal from all our sin and guilt. Because reconciliation has been made for sin, we can now be reconciled to Him. *"God was in Christ reconciling the world unto himself, not imputing their trespasses unto them."* Following this word of reconciliation is the invitation, *"Be ye reconciled to God."* Whoever receives reconciliation for sin, is reconciled to God. He knows that all his sins are forgiven.

The Scriptures use sundry illustrations to emphasize the fullness of forgiveness and to convince the fearful heart of the sinner that the blood has really taken his sin away. *"I have blotted out as a thick cloud thy transgressions, and as a cloud thy sins"* (Isaiah 44:22). *"Thou hast cast all my sins behind thy back"* (Isaiah 38:17). *"Thou wilt cast all their sins into the depths of the sea"* (Micah 7:19). *"The iniquity of Israel shall be sought for and there shall be none; and the sins of Judah and they shall not be found: for I will pardon them"* (Jeremiah 1:20).

This is what the New Testament calls justification. It is thus named in Romans 3:23-26, *"For all have sinned...being justified freely [for nothing] through the redemption that is in Christ Jesus, whom God hath set forth as a reconciliation, through faith in His blood, to declare his righteousness...that he might be just and the justifier of him which believeth in Jesus."*

So perfect is the reconciliation and so really has sin been covered and blotted out, that he who believes in Christ is looked upon, and treated by God, as entirely righteous. The acquittal which he has received from God is so complete that there is nothing, absolutely nothing, to prevent him approaching God with the utmost freedom.

For the enjoyment of this blessedness nothing is necessary save faith in the blood. The blood alone has done everything.

The penitent sinner who turns from his sin to God, needs only faith in that blood. That is, faith in the power of the blood, that it has truly atoned for sin, and that it really has atoned for him. Through that faith, he knows that he is fully reconciled to God, and that there is now not the least thing to hinder God pouring out on him the fullness of His love and blessing.

If he looks towards heaven which formerly was covered with clouds, black with God's wrath, and a coming awful judgment, that cloud is no longer to be seen; everything is bright in the gladsome light of God's face and God's love. Faith in the blood manifests in his heart the same wonder-working power that it exercised in heaven. Through faith in the blood he becomes partaker of all the blessings which the blood has obtained for him from God.

Fellow believers, pray earnestly that the Holy Spirit may reveal to you the glory of this reconciliation, and the pardon of your sins, made yours through the blood of Jesus. Pray for enlightened hearts to see how completely the accusing and condemning power of your sin has been removed, and how God in the fullness of His love and good pleasure has turned towards you. Open your hearts to the Holy Spirit that He may reveal in you the glorious effects which the blood has had in heaven. God hath set forth Jesus Christ Himself as a reconciliation through faith in His blood. He is the reconciliation for our sins. Rely on Him, as having already covered your sin before God. Set Him between yourselves and your sins, and you will experience how complete the redemption is, which He has accomplished, and how powerful the reconciliation is through faith in His blood.

Then through the living Christ, the powerful effects which the blood has exercised in heaven will increasingly be manifested in your hearts, and you will know what it means to walk, by the Spirit's grace, in the full light and enjoyment of forgiveness.

And you who have not yet obtained forgiveness of your sins, does not this word come to you as an urgent call to faith in His blood? Will you never allow yourselves to be moved by what God has done for you as sinners? *"Herein is love, not that we loved God but that He loved us and sent His Son to be the reconciliation for our sins"* (1 John 4:10).

The precious blood divine has been shed; reconciliation is complete; and the message comes to you, *"Be ye reconciled to God."*

If you repent of your sins, and desire to be delivered from sin's power and bondage, exercise faith in the blood. Open your heart to the influence of the word that God has sent to be spoken unto you. Open your heart to the message, that the blood can deliver you—yes, even you—this moment. Only believe it. Say "that blood is also for me." If you come as a guilty, lost sinner, longing for pardon, you may rest assured that the blood, which has already made a perfect reconciliation, covers your sin and restores you, immediately, to the favor and love of God.

So I pray you, exercise faith in the blood. This moment bow down before God, and tell Him that you do believe in the power of the blood for your own soul. Having said that, stand by it; cling to it. Through faith in His blood, Jesus Christ will be the reconciliation for your sins also.

CHAPTER 4

Cleansing through the Blood

*"If we walk in the light, as he is in the light,
we have fellowship one with another, and
the blood of Jesus Christ his Son
cleanseth us from all sin."*
—1 John 1:7

We have seen that the most important effect of the blood is reconciliation for sin.

The fruit of knowledge about, and faith in, reconciliation is the pardon of sin. Pardon is just a declaration of what has already taken place in heaven on the sinner's behalf, and his hearty acceptance of it.

This first effect of the blood is not the only one. In proportion as the soul, through faith, yields itself to the Spirit of God to understand and enjoy the full power of reconciliation, the blood exerts a further power, in the imparting of the other blessings which, in Scripture, are attributed to it.

One of the first results of reconciliation is cleansing from sin. Let us see what God's Word has to say about this. Cleansing is often spoken about, among us, as if it were no more than the pardon of sins, or the cleansing from guilt. This, however, is not so. Scripture does not speak of being cleansed from guilt. Cleansing from sin means deliverance from the pollution, not from the guilt of sin. The guilt of sin concerns our relationship to God, and our responsibility to make good our misdoings (or to bear the punishment of them). The pollution of sin, on the other hand, is the sense of defilement and impurity which sin brings to our inner being, and it is with this that cleansing has to do.

It is of the greatest importance for every believer, who desires to enjoy the full salvation which God has provided for him, to understand aright what the Scriptures teach about this cleansing. Let us consider:

First, what the word cleansing means in the Old Testament;

Second, what is the blessing indicated by that word in the New Testament; and

Third, how may we experience the full enjoyment of this blessing?

Cleansing in the Old Testament

In the service of God as ordained by the hand of Moses for Israel, there were two ceremonies to be observed by God's people in preparation for approach to Him. These were the offerings or sacrifices and the cleansings or purifications. Both were to be observed but in different manners. Both were intended to remind man how sinful he was, and how unfit to draw near to a holy God. Both were to typify the redemption by which the Lord Jesus Christ would restore to man fellowship with God. As a rule it is only the offerings which are regarded as typical of redemption through Christ. The epistle to the Hebrews, however, emphatically mentions the cleansings as figures *"for the time being in which were offered...sacrifices... and divers washings"* (Hebrews 9:9-10).

If we can imagine the life of an Israelite, we shall understand that the consciousness of sin and the need for redemption were awakened not less by the cleansings than the offerings. We must also learn from them what the power of the blood of Jesus actually is.

We may take one of the more important cases of cleansing as an illustration. If anyone was in a hut or house where a dead body lay, or if he had even touched a dead body or bones, he was unclean for seven days. Death, as the punishment for sin, made everyone who came into association with it unclean. Cleansing was accomplished by using the ashes of a young heifer which had been burned, as described in Numbers 19. (Compare Hebrews 9:13-14.) These ashes, mixed with water, were sprinkled by means of a bunch of hyssop on the one who was unclean; he had then to bathe himself in water, after which he was once more ceremonially clean.

The words *unclean, cleansing,* and *clean* were used in reference to the healing of leprosy, a disease which might be described as a living death. Here also he who was to be cleansed must bathe in water, having been first sprinkled with water, in which the blood of a bird, sacrificially offered, had been mixed. Seven days later he was again sprinkled with sacrificial blood (Leviticus, chapters 13 and 14).

An attentive contemplation of the laws of cleansing will teach us that the difference between the cleansings and the offerings was twofold. First, the offering had definite reference to the transgression for which reconciliation had to be made. Cleansing had more to do with conditions which were not sinful in themselves, but were the result of sin, and therefore must be acknowledged by God's holy people as defiled. Secondly, in the case of the offering, nothing was done to the offerer himself. He saw the blood sprinkled on the altar or carried into the Holy Place; he must believe that this procures reconciliation before God. But nothing was done to himself. In cleansing, on the other hand, what happened to the person was the chief thing. Defilement was something that, either through internal disease or outward touch, had come upon the man; so the washing or sprinkling with water must take place on himself as ordained by God.

Cleansing was something that he could feel and experience. It brought about a change not only in his relationship to God, but in his own condition. In the offering something was done for him; by cleansing something was done in him. The offering had respect to his guilt; the cleansing, to the pollution of sin.

The same meaning of the words *clean* and *cleansing* is found elsewhere in the Old Testament. David prays in Psalm 51, *"Cleanse me from my sin...Purge me with hyssop and I shall be clean."* The word used by David here is that which is used most frequently for the cleansing of anyone who had touched a dead body. Hyssop also was used in such cases. David prayed for more than pardon. He confessed that he had been *"shapen in iniquity,"* that his nature was sinful. He prayed that he might be made pure within. *"Cleanse me from my sin,"* was his prayer. He uses the same word later on when he prays, *"Create in me a clean heart, O God."* Cleansing is more than pardon.

In the same manner, this word is used by Ezekiel and refers to an inner condition which must be changed. This is evident from chapter 24, verses 11 and 13, where, speaking of uncleanness being melted out, God says: *"Because I have purged thee and thou wast not purged."* Later on in Ezekiel 36:25, speaking of the New Covenant, He says, *"Then will I sprinkle clean water upon you, and ye shall be clean: from all your filthiness, and from all your idols, will I cleanse you."*

Malachi uses the same word, connecting it with fire, *"He shall sit as a refiner and purifier of silver, he shall purify [cleanse] the sons of Levi"* (Malachi 3:3).

Cleansing by water, by blood, by fire are all typical of the cleansing which would take place under the New Covenant—an inner cleansing and deliverance from the stain of sin.

Cleansing as Blessing in the New Testament

Mention is often made in the New Testament of a clean or pure heart. Our Lord said, *"Blessed are the pure in heart"* (Matthew 5:8).

Paul speaks of *"love out of a pure heart"* (1 Timothy 1:5). He speaks also of a *"pure conscience."*

Peter exhorts his readers to *"love one another with a pure heart fervently."* The word cleansing is also used.

We read of those who are described as God's people that God purified (cleansed) their hearts through faith (Acts 15:9).

That the purpose of the Lord Jesus concerning those who were His was *"to purify [cleanse] to himself a people of his own possession"* (Titus 2:14).

Regarding ourselves we read, *"Let us cleanse ourselves from all filthiness of the flesh and spirit"* (2 Corinthians 7:1).

All these places teach us that cleansing is an inward work wrought in the heart and that it is subsequent to pardon.

We are told in 1 John 1:7 that *"the blood of Jesus Christ his Son cleanseth us from all sin."* This word *cleanseth* does not refer to the grace of pardon received at conversion, but to the effect of grace in God's children who walk in the light. We read, *"If we walk in the light as he is in the light...the blood of Jesus Christ his Son cleanseth us from all sin."* That it refers to something more than pardon appears from what follows in verse 9: *"He is faithful and just to forgive us our sins and to cleanse us from all unrighteousness."* Cleansing is something that comes after pardon and is the result of it, by the inward and experiential reception of the power of the blood of Jesus in the heart of the believer.

This takes place according to the Word, first in the purifying of the conscience. *"How much more shall the blood of Christ...purge your conscience from dead works to serve the living God"* (Hebrews 9:14). The mention already made of the ashes of an heifer sprinkling the unclean typifies a personal experience of the precious blood of Christ. Conscience is not only a judge to give sentence on our actions; it is also the inward voice which bears witness to our relationship to God, and to God's relationship to us. When it is cleansed by the blood then it bears witness that we are well pleasing to God.

It is written in Hebrews 10:2, *"The worshipers once purged should have no more conscience of sins."* We receive through the Spirit an inward experience that the blood has so fully delivered us from the guilt and power of sin that we, in our regenerated nature, have escaped entirely from its dominion. Sin still dwells in our flesh, with its temptations, but it has no power to rule. The conscience is cleansed; there is no need for the least shadow of separation between God and us; we look up to Him in the full power of redemption. The conscience cleansed by the blood bears witness to nothing less than a complete redemption; the fullness of God's good pleasure.

And if the conscience is cleansed so also is the heart, of which the conscience is the center. We read of having the heart cleansed from an evil conscience (Hebrews 10:22). Not only must the conscience be cleansed, but the heart also must be cleansed, including the understanding and the will, with all our thoughts and desires. Through the blood, by the shedding of which Christ delivered Himself up to death, and by virtue of which He entered again into heaven, the death and resurrection of Christ are ceaselessly effectual. By this power of His death and resurrection, sinful lusts and dispositions are slain.

"The blood of Jesus Christ cleanseth from all sin," from original, as well as from actual, sin. The blood exercises its spiritual, heavenly power in the soul. The believer in whose life the blood is fully efficacious, experiences that the old nature is hindered from manifesting its power. Through the blood, its lusts and desires are subdued and slain, and everything is cleansed that the Spirit can bring forth His glorious fruit. In case of the least stumbling, the soul finds immediate cleansing and restoration. Even unconscious sins are rendered powerless through its efficacy.

We have noted a difference between the guilt and the pollution of sin. This is of importance for a clear understanding of the matter, but in actual life, we must ever remember that they are not thus divided. God through the blood deals with sin as a whole. Every true operation of the blood manifests its power simultaneously over the guilt and the pollution of sin. Reconciliation and cleansing always go together, and the blood is ceaselessly operative.

Many seem to think that the blood is there, so that if we have sinned again, we can turn again to it to be cleansed. But this is not so. Just as a fountain flows always, and always purifies what is placed in it or under its stream, so it is with this fountain, opened for sin and uncleanness (Zechariah 13:1). The eternal power of life of the Eternal Spirit works through the blood. Through Him the heart can abide always under the flow and cleansing of the blood.

In the Old Testament cleansing was necessary for each sin. In the New Testament cleansing depends on Him who ever lives to intercede. When faith sees and desires and lays hold of this fact, the heart can abide every moment under the protecting and cleansing power of the blood.

Experiencing the Full Enjoyment of This Blessing

Everyone, who through faith obtains a share in the atoning merit of the blood of

Christ, has a share in its cleansing efficacy also. But the experience of its power to cleanse is, for several reasons, sadly imperfect. It is therefore of great importance to understand what the conditions are for the full enjoyment of this glorious blessing.

First of all, knowledge is necessary. Many think that pardon of sin is all that we receive through the blood. They ask for and so obtain nothing more.

It is a blessed thing to begin to see that the Holy Spirit of God has a special purpose in making use of different words in Scripture concerning the effects of the blood. Then we begin to inquire about their special meaning. Let everyone who truly longs to know what the Lord desires to teach us by this one word cleansing, attentively compare all the places in Scripture where the word is used, where cleansing is spoken of. He will soon feel that there is more promised to the believer than the removal of guilt. He will begin to understand that cleansing through washing can take away stain, and although he cannot fully explain in what way this takes place, he will, however, be convinced that he may expect a blessed inward operation of the cleansing away of the effects of sin by the blood. Knowledge of this fact is the first condition of experiencing it.

Secondly, there must be desire. It is to be feared that our Christianity is only too pleased to postpone to a future life the experience of the Beatitude which our Lord intended for our earthly life: *"Blessed are the pure in heart, for they shall see God."*

It is not sufficiently recognized that purity of heart is a characteristic of every child of God, because it is the necessary condition of fellowship with Him, of the enjoyment of His salvation. There is too little inner longing to be really in all things, at all times, well pleasing to the Lord. Sin and the stain of sin trouble us too little.

God's Word comes to us with the promise of blessing which ought to awaken all our desires. Believe that the blood of Jesus cleanses from all sin. If you learn how to yield yourself rightly to its operation it can do great things in you. Should you not every hour desire to experience its glorious cleansing efficacy; to be preserved, in spite of your depraved nature, from the many stains for which your conscience is constantly accusing you? May your desires be awakened to long for this blessing. Put God to the test to work out in you what He as the Faithful One has promised, *"cleansing from all unrighteousness."*

The third condition is a willingness to separate yourself from everything that is unclean. Through sin, everything in our nature and in the world is defiled. Cleansing cannot take place where there is not an entire separation from, and giving up of, everything unclean. *"Touch not the unclean thing"* is God's command to His chosen ones. I must recognize that all the things surrounding me are unclean.

My friends, my possessions, my spirit must all be surrendered that I may be cleansed in each relationship by the precious blood, and that all the activities of my spirit, soul, and being may experience a thorough cleansing.

He who will keep back anything however small cannot obtain the full blessing. He who is willing to pay the full price so as to have his whole being baptized by the blood is on the way to understand fully this word: *"The blood of Jesus cleanseth from all sin."*

The last condition is exercising faith in the power of the blood. It is not as if we, through our faith, bestow its efficacy upon the blood. No, the blood ever retains its power and efficacy, but our unbelief closes our hearts and hinders its operation. Faith is simply the removal of that hindrance, the setting open of our hearts, for the divine power by which the living Lord will bestow His blood.

Yes, let us believe that there is cleansing through the blood.

You have perhaps seen a spring in the midst of a patch of grass. From the much traveled road that runs by that patch, dust is constantly falling over the grass that grows by the side of the road. But where the water from the spring falls in refreshing and cleansing spray, there is no sign of dust, and everything is green and fresh. So the precious blood of Christ carries on its blessed work without ceasing in the soul of the believer who by faith appropriates it. He who by faith commits himself to the Lord and believes that this can and will take place, it will be given to him.

The heavenly, spiritual effect of the blood can be really experienced every moment. Its power is such that I can always abide in the fountain, always dwell in the wounds of my Lord.

Believer, come, I entreat of you; put it to the proof how the blood of Jesus can cleanse your heart from all sin.

You know with what joy a weary traveler would bathe in a fresh stream, plunging into the water to experience its cooling, cleansing, strengthening effect. Lift up your eyes and see by faith how ceaselessly a stream flows from heaven above to earth beneath. It is the blessed Spirit's influence, through whom the power of the blood of Jesus flows earthwards over souls, to heal and to purify them. Oh, place yourself in this stream; simply believe that the words *"The blood of Jesus cleanseth from all sin"* have a divine meaning—deeper, wider, than you have ever imagined. Believe that it is the Lord Jesus Himself who will cleanse you in His blood, and fulfill His promise in power in you. And reckon on the cleansing from sin by His blood, as a blessing, in the daily enjoyment of which you can confidently abide.

CHAPTER 5

Sanctification through the Blood

*"Wherefore Jesus also, that he might sanctify
the people with his own blood,
suffered without the gate."*
—Hebrews 13:12

"Cleansing through the blood" was the subject of our last chapter. Sanctification through the blood must now occupy our attention.

To a superficial observer it might seem that there is little difference between cleansing and sanctification, that the two words mean about the same thing. But the difference is great and important. Cleansing has to do chiefly with the old life, and the stain of sin which must be removed, and is only preparatory. Sanctification concerns the new life and that characteristic of it which must be imparted to it by God. Sanctification, which means union with God, is the peculiar fullness of blessing purchased for us by the blood.

The distinction between these two things is clearly marked in Scripture. Paul reminds us that *"Christ...gave himself for the church... that he might sanctify it, having cleansed it"* (Ephesians 5:25-26). Having first cleansed it, then He sanctifies it. Writing to Timothy he says, *"If a man therefore purge himself from these, he shall be a vessel unto honor, sanctified, and meet for the master's use"* (2 Timothy 2:21). Sanctification is a blessing which follows after, and surpasses, cleansing.

It is also strikingly illustrated by the ordinances connected with the consecration of the priests compared with that of the Levites. In the case of the latter, who took a lower position than the priests in the service of the sanctuary, no mention is made of sanctification, but the term *cleansing* is used five times (Numbers 13). In the consecration of the priests, on the other hand, the word *sanctify* is often used, for the priests stood in a closer relationship to God than the Levites (Exodus 29; Leviticus 8).

This record at the same time emphasizes the close connection between the sacrificial blood, and sanctification. In the case of the consecration of the Levites, reconciliation for sin was made, and they were sprinkled with the water of purification for cleansing, but they were not sprinkled with blood. But in the consecration of the priests, blood had to be sprinkled upon them. They were sanctified by a more personal and intimate application of the blood.

All this was typical of sanctification through the blood of Jesus, and this is what we now seek to understand, that we may obtain a share in it. Let us then consider:

First, what sanctification is;

Second, that it was the great object of the sufferings of Christ; and

Last, that it can be obtained through the blood.

What Sanctification Is

To understand what the sanctification of the redeemed is, we must first learn what the holiness of God is. He alone is the Holy One. Holiness in the creature must be received from Him.

God's holiness is often spoken of as though it consisted in His hatred of, and hostility to, sin; but this gives no explanation of what holiness actually is. It is a merely negative statement—-that God's holiness cannot bear sin.

Holiness is that attribute of God, because of which, He always is and wills and does what is supremely good; because of which also, He desires what is supremely good in His creatures and bestows it upon them.

God is called *"the Holy One"* in Scripture, not only because He punishes sin, but also because He is the Redeemer of His people. It is His holiness, which ever wills what is good for all, that moved Him to redeem sinners. Both the wrath of God which punishes sin and love of God which redeems the sinner spring from the same source—His holiness. Holiness is the perfection of God's nature.

Holiness in man is a disposition in entire agreement with that of God, which chooses in all things to will as God wills, as it is written: *"As he is holy, so be ye holy"* (1 Peter 1:15). Holiness in us is nothing else than oneness with God. The sanctification of God's people is effected by the communication to them of the holines of God. There is no way of obtaining sanctification, save by the Holy God bestowing what He alone possesses. He alone is the Holy One. He is the Lord who sanctifies.

By the different meanings which Scripture attaches to the words *sanctification* and *to sanctify,* a certain relationship with God, into which we are brought, is pointed out.

The first and simplest meaning of the word *sanctification* is separation. That which is taken out of its surroundings, by God's command, and is set aside or separated as His own possession and for His service—that is holy. This does not mean separation from sin only, but from all that is in the world, even from what may be permissible. Thus God sanctified the seventh day. The other days were not unclean, for God saw all that He had made and *beheld it was very good.* But that day alone was holy which God had taken possession of by His own special act. In the same way, God had separated Israel from other nations, and in Israel had separated the priests, to be holy unto Him. This separation unto sanctification is always God's own work, and so the electing grace of God is often closely connected with sanctification. *"Ye shall be holy unto me...I have separated you...that ye should be mine"* (Leviticus 20:26). *"The man whom the Lord shall choose shall be holy"* (Numbers 16:7). *"Thou art an holy people unto the Lord, the Lord thy God hath chosen thee"* (Deuteronomy 7:6). God cannot take part with other lords. He must be the sole possessor and ruler of those to whom He reveals and imparts His holiness.

But this separation is not all that is included in the word *sanctification.* It is only the indispensable condition of what must follow. When separated, man stands before God in no respect differing from an object without life that has been sanctified to the service of God. If the separation is to be of value, something more must take place. Man must surrender himself willingly and heartily to this separation. Sanctification includes personal consecration to the Lord to be His.

Sanctification can become ours only when it sends down its roots into and takes up its abode in the depths of our personal life, in our will, and in our love. God sanctifies no man against his will; therefore, the personal, hearty surrender to God is an indispensable part of sanctification.

It is for this reason that the Scriptures not only speak of God sanctifying us, but they say often that we must sanctify ourselves.

But even by consecration, true sanctification is not yet complete. Separation and consecration are together only the preparation for the glorious work that God will do, as He imparts His own holiness to the soul. *"Partaking of the divine nature"* is the blessing which is promised to believers in sanctification. *"That we might be partakers of his holiness"* (Hebrews 12:10). That is the glorious aim of God's work in those whom He separates for Himself. But this impartation of His holiness is not a gift of something that is apart from God Himself. No! It is in personal fellowship with Him, and partaking of His divine life, that sanctification can be obtained.

As the Holy One, God dwelt among the people of Israel to sanctify his people (Exodus 29:45-46). As the Holy One, He dwells in us. It is the presence of God alone that can sanctify. But so surely is this our portion, that Scripture does not shrink from speaking of God dwelling in our hearts in such power that we may be *filled unto all the fullness of God.*" True sanctification is fellowship with God and His dwelling in us. So it was necessary that God in Christ should take up His abode in the flesh, and that the Holy Spirit should come to dwell in us. This is what sanctification means.

Sanctification as the Object for Which Christ Suffered

This is plainly stated in Hebrews 13:12: *"Jesus suffered that he might sanctify his people."* In the wisdom of God a participation in His holiness is the highest destiny of man. Therefore, also, this was the central object of the coming of our Lord Jesus to earth; and above all, of His sufferings and death. It was *"that he might sanctify his people"* and *"that they might be holy and without blame"* (Ephesians 1:4).

How the sufferings of Christ attained this end, and became our sanctification, is made plain to us by the words which He spoke to His

Father, when He was about to allow Himself to be bound as a sacrifice. *"For their sakes I sanctify myself that they also may be sanctified through the truth"* (John 17:19). It was because His sufferings and death were a sanctification of Himself, that they can become sanctification for us.

What does that mean? Jesus was *"the Holy One of God,"* *"The Son whom the Father had sanctified and sent into the world,"* and must He sanctify Himself? He must do so; it was indispensable.

The sanctification which He possessed was not beyond the reach of temptation. In His temptation He must maintain it, and show how perfectly His will was surrendered to the holiness of God. We have seen that true holiness in man is the perfect oneness of His will with that of God. Through all our Lord's life, from the temptation in the wilderness onwards, He had subjected His will to the will of His Father, and had consecrated Himself as a sacrifice to God. But it was chiefly in Gethsemane He did this. There was the hour and the power of darkness; the temptation to put away the terrible cup of wrath from His lips and to do His own will came with almost irresistible power, but He rejected the temptation. He offered up Himself and His will to the will and holiness of God. He sanctified Himself by a perfect oneness of will with that of God. This sanctification of Himself has become the power by which we also may be sanctified through the truth. This is in perfect accord with what we learn from the epistle to the Hebrews where, speaking of the words used by Christ, we read, *"I come to do thy will, O God,"* and then it is added, *"By the which will we are sanctified by the offering of the body of Jesus Christ once for all"* (Hebrews 10:9-10). It was because the offering of His body was His surrender of Himself to do the will of God that we become sanctified by that will. He sanctified Himself there for us that we might be sanctified through the truth. The perfect obedience in which He surrendered Himself, that God's holy will might be accomplished in Him, was not only the meritorious cause of our salvation, but is at the same time the power by which sin was forever conquered, and by which the same disposition, and the same sanctification, may be created in our hearts.

Elsewhere in this epistle to the Hebrews, the true relationship of our Lord to His own people is even more clearly characterized as having sanctification for its chief end—after speaking of how becoming it was that our Lord should suffer as He did we read: *"For both he that sanctifieth, and they who are sanctified, are all of one"* (Hebrews 2:11). The unity between the Lord Jesus and His people consists in the fact that they both receive their life from one Father, and both have a share in one and the same sanctification. Jesus is the sanctifier, they become the sanctified. Sanctification is the bond that unites them. *"Therefore Jesus also suffered that he might sanctify his people with his own blood."*

If we are willing really to understand and experience what sanctification by the blood means, then it is of the utmost importance for us, first to lay fast hold of the fact that sanctification is the characteristic and purpose of the entire sufferings of our Lord, of which sufferings the blood was the fruit and means of blessing. His sanctification of Himself has the characteristic of those sufferings, and therein lay its value and power. Our sanctification is the purpose of those sufferings, and only to attain that purpose do they work out the perfect blessing. In proportion as this is clear to us, we shall press forward into the true meaning and blessing of His sufferings.

It was as the Holy One that God foreordained redemption. It was His will to glorify His holiness in victory over sin by the sanctification of man after His own image. It was with the same object that our Lord Jesus endured and accomplished His sufferings; we must be consecrated to God. And if the Holy Spirit, the holy God as Spirit—comes into us to reveal in us the redemption that is in Jesus, this continues to be with Him also the main object. As the Holy Spirit, He is the spirit of holiness.

Reconciliation, pardon, and cleansing from sin have all an unspeakable value; they all, however, point onwards to sanctification. It is God's will that each one who has been marked by the precious blood should know that it is a divine mark, characterizing his entire separation to God; that this blood calls him to an undivided consecration to a life wholly for God; and that this blood is the promise and the power of a participation in God's holiness, through which God Himself will make His abiding place in him and be his God.

Oh, that we might understand and believe that *Jesus also suffered, that he might sanctify his people with his own blood"* (Hebrews 13:12).

How to Obtain Sanctification by the Blood

An answer to this question, in general, is that every one who is a partaker of the virtue of the blood, is also a partaker of sanctification, and is in God's sight a sanctified person.

In proportion as he lives in close and abiding contact with the blood, he continues to experience, increasingly, its sanctifying effects; even though he still understands but little of how those effects are produced. Let no one think that he must first understand how to lay hold of or explain everything, before he may, by faith, pray that the blood might manifest its sanctifying power in him. No, it was just in connection with the bath of cleansing—the washing of the disciples' feet—that the Lord Jesus said, *"What I do thou knowest not now but thou shalt know hereafter."* It is the Lord Jesus Himself who sanctifies His people *"by His own blood."* He who heartily gives himself up to believing worship of and intimacy with the Lamb, who has bought us with His blood, will experience through that blood a sanctification beyond his conception. The Lord Jesus will do this for him.

But the believer ought to grow in knowledge also; thus only can he enter into the full blessing which is prepared for him. We have not only the right, but it is our duty to inquire earnestly what the essential connection is between the blessed effect of the blood and our sanctification, and in what way the Lord Jesus will work out in us, by His blood, those things which we have ascertained to be the chief qualities of sanctification.

We have seen that the beginning of all sanctification is separation to God, as His entire possession, to be at His disposal. This is just what the blood proclaims: that the power of sin is broken; that we are loosed from its bonds; that we are no longer its bond-servants, but belong to Him who purchased our freedom with His blood. *"Ye are not your own, ye are bought with a price."* This is the language in which the blood tells us that we are God's possession. Because He desires to have us entirely for Himself, He has chosen and bought us, and set upon us the distinguishing mark of the blood, as those who are separated from all around them, to live only for His service. This idea of separation is clearly expressed in the words we so often repeat, *"Jesus, that he might sanctify his people with his own blood, suffered without the gate. Let us go forth therefore unto him without the camp bearing his reproach"* (Hebrews 13:12-13). *"Going out"* from all that is of this world was the characteristic of Him who was holy, undefiled, separate from sinners; and it must also be the characteristic of all His followers.

Believer, the Lord Jesus has sanctified you through His own blood, and He desires to make you experience, through that blood, the full power of this sanctification. Endeavor to gain a clear impression of what has taken place in you through the sprinkling of that blood. The holy God desires to have you entirely for Himself. No one, nothing, may any longer have the least right over you, nor have you any right over yourself. God has separated you unto Himself, and that you might feel this, He set His mark upon you. That mark is the most wonderful thing that is to be found on earth or in heaven—the blood of Jesus. The blood in which the life of the eternal Son of God is, the blood that on the throne of grace is ever before God's face, the blood that assures you of full redemption from the power of sin—that blood is sprinkled upon you as a sign that you belong to God.

Believer, I pray you, let every thought about the blood awaken in you the glorious confession, "By his own blood, the Lord Jesus has sanctified me, he has taken complete possession of me for God, and I belong entirely to God."

We have seen that sanctification is more than separation. That is only the beginning. We have seen also that personal consecration and hearty and willing surrender to live only for and in God's holy will is part of sanctification.

In what way can the blood of Christ work out this surrender in us and sanctify us in that surrender? The answer is not difficult. It is not enough to believe in the power of the blood to redeem us and to free us from sin, but we must, above all, notice the source of this power.

We know that it has this power, because of the willingness with which the Lord Jesus surrendered Himself. In the shedding of His blood He sanctified Himself, offered Himself entirely to God and His holiness. It is because of this that the blood is so holy, and possesses such sanctifying power. In the blood we have an impressive representation of the utter self-surrender of Christ. The blood ever speaks of the consecration of Jesus to the Father, as the opening of the way to, and supplying the power for, victory over sin. The closer we come into contact with the blood, and the more we live under the deep impression of having been sprinkled by the blood, we shall hear more clearly the voice of the blood declaring, "Entire surrender to God is the way to full redemption from sin."

The voice of the blood will not speak simply to teach us or to awaken thought; the blood speaks with a divine and life-giving power. What it commands, that it bestows. It works out in us the same disposition that was in our Lord Jesus. By His own blood Jesus sanctifies us, that we, holding nothing back, might surrender ourselves with all our hearts to the holy will of God.

But consecration itself even along with and following separation is still only a preparation. Entire sanctification takes place when God takes possession of and fills with His glory the temple that is consecrated to Him. *There will I meet with the children of Israel, and they shall be sanctified by my glory* (Exodus 29:43). Actual, complete sanctification consists in God's impartation of His own holiness—of Himself.

Here also the blood speaks: it tells us that heaven is opened, that the powers of the heavenly life have come down to earth, that every hindrance has been removed. God can make His abode with man.

Immediate nearness and fellowship with God are made possible by the blood. The believer who surrenders himself unreservedly to the blood obtains the full assurance that God will bestow Himself wholly and will reveal His holiness in him.

How glorious are the results of such a sanctification! Through the Holy Spirit, the soul's intimacy is in the living experience of God's abiding nearness, accompanied by the awakening of the tenderest carefulness against sin, guarded by caution and the fear of God.

But to live in watchfulness against sin does not satisfy the soul. The temple must not only be cleansed, but it must be filled with God's glory. All the virtues of divine holiness, as manifested in the Lord Jesus, are to be sought for and found in fellowship with God. Sanctification means union with God, fellowship in His will, sharing His life, conformity to His image.

Christians, *"wherefore Jesus also...suffered without the gate that he might sanctify his people with his own blood. Let us go forth unto him without the camp."* Yes, it is He who sanctifies His people. *"Let us go forth unto him."* Let us trust Him to make known to us the power of the blood. Let us yield ourselves wholly to its blessed efficacy. That blood, through which He sanctified Himself, has entered heaven to open it for us. It can make our hearts also a throne of God, that the grace and glory of God may dwell in us. Yes, *let us go forth unto him without the camp.*" He who is willing to lose and say farewell to everything, in order that Jesus may sanctify him, will not fail to obtain the blessing. He who is willing at any cost to experience the full power of the precious blood can confidently reckon that he will be sanctified by Jesus Himself, through that blood.

"The very God of peace sanctify you wholly." Amen.

CHAPTER 6

Cleansed by the Blood to Serve the Living God

"Now in Christ Jesus ye who sometimes were far off are made nigh by the blood of Christ."
—*Ephesians 2:13*

*"How much more shall the blood of Christ
...purge your conscience...
to serve the living God?"*
—*Hebrews 9:14*

After our study of sanctification through the blood, we are now to be engaged in the consideration of what the intimate relationship with God into which we are introduced by sanctification, involves.

Sanctification and intimacy are closely related facts in Scripture. Apart from sanctification there can be no such relationship. How could one who is unholy have fellowship with a holy God? On the other hand, without this relationship there can be no growth in holiness; it is always and only in fellowship with the Holy One, that holiness can be found.

The intimate connection between sanctification and relationship appears plainly in the story of the revolt of Nadab and Abihu. God made this the occasion of a clear statement concerning the peculiar nature of the priesthood in Israel. He said, *"I will be sanctified in them that come nigh me"* (Leviticus 10:3). Then again in the conspiracy of Korah against Moses and Aaron, Moses speaking for God said, *"Tomorrow the Lord shall show who are his, and who is holy: and will cause him to come near unto him, even him whom he hath chosen, will he cause to come near unto him"* (Numbers 16:5).

We have already seen that God's election and separation unto Himself of His own, are closely bound up with sanctification. It is evident here, also, that the glory and blessing secured by this election to holiness, is nothing else than intimacy with God. This is indeed the highest, the one perfect blessing for man, who was created for God, and to enjoy His love. The Psalmist sings, *"Blessed is the man whom thou choosest, and causest to approach unto thee, that he may dwell in thy courts"* (Psalm 65:4). In the nature of the case, consecration to God and nearness to Him are the same thing.

The sprinkling of the blood, which sanctifies man unto God and takes possession of him for God, bestows at the same time the right of intimacy.

It was thus with the priests in Israel. In the record of their consecration we read, *"And Moses brought Aaron's sons, and Moses put of the blood upon the tip of their right ear, and upon the thumbs of their right hands"* (Leviticus 8:24). Those who belong to God may, and indeed must, live in nearness to Him; they belong to Him. This is illustrated in the case of our Lord, our great High Priest, who *"through his own blood entered, once for all, into the holy place."* It is the same with every believer, according to the Word, *"Having therefore, brethren, boldness to enter into the holiest by the blood of Jesus...let us draw near, having our hearts sprinkled from an evil conscience"* (Hebrews 10:19, 22). The word *enter,* as used in this verse, is the peculiar word used of the approach of the priest to God. In the same way, in the book of Revelation, our right to draw near as priests is declared to be by the power of the blood. We were *"redeemed from our sins by his own blood"* who *"has made us kings and priests unto God...to him be the glory for ever"* (Revelation 10:9, 10). *"These are they...who have washed their robes and made them white in the blood of the Lamb, therefore are they before the throne of God and serve him day and night in his temple"* (Revelation 7:14).

One of the most glorious blessings made possible for us by the power of the blood is that of drawing near the throne into the very presence of God. That we may understand what this blessing means, let us consider what is contained in it. It includes:

First, the right to dwell in the presence of God;

Second, the vocation of offering spiritual sacrifices to God; and

Third, the power to procure blessing for others.

The Right to Dwell in the Presence of God

Although this privilege belonged exclusively to the priests in Israel, we know that they had free access to the dwelling place of God. They had to abide there continually. As members of the household of God, they ate the shewbread, and partook of the sacrifices. A true Israelite thought there was no higher privilege than this. It is thus expressed by the psalmist, *"Blessed [happy] is the man whom thou*

*choosest, and causest to approach unto thee that
he may dwell in thy courts. We shall be satisfied with the goodness of thy house, even of thy
holy temple"* (Psalm 65:4).

It was because of the manifested presence
of God there that believers, in those old days,
longed after the house of God with such strong
desire. The cry was, *"When shall I come and
appear before God?"* (Psalm 42:2). They understood something of the spiritual meaning of the
privilege, "drawing near to God." It represented
to them the enjoyment of His love, and fellowship, and protection, and blessing. They could
exclaim, *"Oh, how great is thy goodness which
thou hast laid up for them that fear thee...thou
shalt hide them in the secret of thy presence"*
(Psalm 31:19, 20).

The precious blood of Christ has opened
the way for the believer into God's presence;
and intimacy with Him is a deep, spiritual
reality. He who knows the full power of the
blood is brought so nigh that he can always
live in the immediate presence of God and in
the enjoyment of the unspeakable blessings
attached to it. There, the child of God has the
assurance of God's love; he experiences and
enjoys it. God Himself imparts it. He lives daily
in the friendship and fellowship of God. As
God's child he makes known to the Father,
with perfect freedom, his thoughts and wishes.
In this intimacy with God, he possesses all that

he needs; he wants no good thing. His soul is kept in perfect rest and peace, because God is with him. He receives all requisite direction and teaching. God's eye is ever upon him, guiding him. In intimacy with God, he is able to hear the softest whispers of the Holy Spirit. He learns to understand the slightest sign of his Father's will and to follow it. His strength continually increases, for God is his strength; and God is ever with him.

Fellowship with God exercises a wonderful influence on his life and character. The presence of God fills him with humility, and fear, and a holy circumspection. He lives as in the presence of a king. Fellowship with God produces in him godlike dispositions. Beholding the image of God, he is changed into the same image. Dwelling with the Holy One makes him holy He can say, *"It is good for me to draw nigh to God"* (Psalm 73:28).

Oh, you who are the children of the New Covenant, have not you a thousand times more reason to speak thus, now that the veil has been torn asunder and the way opened for living always in God's holy presence? May this high privilege awaken our desires. Intimacy with God, fellowship with God, dwelling with God and He with us—may it become impossible for us to be satisfied with anything less. This is the true Christian life.

But relationship with God is not only so blessed because of the salvation enjoyed in it, but also on account of the service that may be rendered, because of that intimacy. Let us therefore consider:

The Vocation of Offering Spiritual Sacrifices to God

Our vocation to bring to God spiritual sacrifices is a further privilege.

The enjoyment of the priests in drawing near to God in His dwelling place was subordinated entirely to something higher. They were there as servants of the Holy Place, to bring to God, in His house, that which belonged to Him. Only as they found joy in drawing near to God, could that service become truly blessed.

The service consisted in the bringing in of the blood of sprinkling; the preparation of the incense to fill the house with its fragrance; and, further, in the ordering of everything that pertained, according to God's word, to the arrangement of His house.

They must so guard and serve and provide for the dwelling place of the Most High, that it should be worthy of Him, and of His glory, and that His good pleasure in it might be fulfilled.

If the blood of Jesus brings us near, it is also, chiefly, that we should live before God as

His servants, and bring to Him the spiritual sacrifices which are well pleasing in His sight.

The priests brought the blood into the Holy Place before God. In our relationship with God, there is no offering that we can bring more pleasing to Him than a believing honoring of the blood of the Lamb. Every act of humble trust or of hearty thanksgiving, in which we direct the attention of the Father to the blood, and speak its praises, is acceptable to Him. Our whole abiding there, and intimacy, from hour to hour must be a glorifying of the blood before God.

The priests brought the incense into the Holy Place, so as to fill God's house with fragrance. The prayers of God's people are the delightful incense with which He desires to be surrounded in His habitation. The value of prayer does not consist merely in its being the means of obtaining things we need. No! It has a higher aim than that. It is a ministry of God in which He delights.

The life of a believer who truly enjoys drawing near to God through the blood is a life of unceasing prayer. In a deep sense of dependence, for each moment, for each step, grace is sought for and expected. In the blessed conviction of God's nearness and unchanging goodness, the soul pours itself out in the confident assurance of faith that every promise will be fulfilled. In the midst of the joy which the light of God's face bestows, there arises at the same time, along with prayer, thanksgiving, and adoration.

These are the spiritual offerings—the offerings of the lips of the priests of God—continually presented to Him. They having been sanctified and brought nigh by the blood that they might ever live and walk in His presence.

But there is still something more. It was the duty of the priests to attend to everything for cleansing or provision that was necessary in the ministry of the house. What is the ministry now under the New Covenant? Thanks be to God, there are no outward nor exclusive arrangements for divine worship. No! The Father has so ordered that whatever any one does who is walking in His presence, just because of that, it becomes a spiritual offering. Everything the believer does, if only he does it as in God's presence and as inspired by the priestly disposition, which offers it to God as a service, it is a priestly sacrifice, well pleasing to God. *"Whether therefore ye eat or drink or whatever ye do, do all to the glory of God"* (1 Corinthians 10:31). *"Whatsoever ye do in word or deed, do all in the name of the Lord Jesus, giving thanks to God and the Father by him"* (Colossians 3:17). In this way, all our actions become thank offerings to God.

How little Christians recognize the glory of a life of complete consecration to be spent always in intimacy with God!

Cleansed, sanctified, and brought nigh by the power of the blood, my earthly calling, my whole life, even my eating and drinking are a spiritual service. My work, my business, my money, my house, and everything with which I have to do becomes sanctified by the presence of God, because I, myself, walk in His presence. The poorest earthly work is a priestly service, because it is performed by a priest of God's temple.

But even this does not exhaust the glory of the blessing of intimacy. The highest blessing of the priesthood is, that the priest appears as the representative of others before God.

The Power to Procure Blessing for Others

This is what gives to nearness to God its full glory.

In Israel the priests were the mediators between God and the people. They carried into the presence of God the sins and needs of the people: they obtained from God the power to declare the pardon of sin and the right of blessing the people.

This privilege now belongs to all believers, as the priestly family of the New Covenant. When God permitted His redeemed ones to approach Him through the blood, it was that He might bless them in order that they might become a blessing to others. Priestly mediation; a priestly heart that can have the needed sympathy with those who are weak; a priestly power to obtain the blessing of God in the temple and convey it to others—in these things, intimacy, the drawing near to God through the blood, manifests its highest power and glory.

We can exercise our priestly dignity in a twofold manner: first, by intercession, and second, instrumentally.

By Intercession

The ministry of intercession is one of the highest privileges of the child of God. It does not mean that in this ministry we, having ascertained that there is a need in the world or in some particular person, pour out our wishes in prayer to God, asking for the necessary supply. That is good, so far as it goes, and brings a blessing with it. But the peculiar ministry of intercession is something more wonderful than that and finds its power in *"the prayer of faith."* This *"prayer of faith"* is a different thing from the outpouring of our wishes to God, and leaving them with Him.

In the true *"prayer of faith,"* the intercessor must spend time with God to appropriate the promises of His Word, and must permit himself to be taught by the Holy Spirit whether the promises can be applied to this particular case. He takes upon himself as a burden, the sin and need which are the subject of prayer, and lays fast hold of the promise concerning it, as though it were for himself. He remains in the presence of God, till God by His Spirit awakens the faith that in this matter the prayer has been heard. In this way parents sometimes pray for their children, ministers for their congregations, laborers in God's vineyard for the souls committed to them, till they know that their prayer is heard. It is the blood that, by its power of bringing us near to God, bestows such wonderful liberty to pray until the answer is obtained.

Oh! If we understood more perfectly what it really means to dwell in the presence of God, we should manifest more power in the exercise of our holy priesthood.

As Instruments

A further manifestation of our priestly mediation is that we not only obtain some blessing for others by intercession, but become the instruments by whom it is ministered. Every believer is called and feels himself compelled by love to labor on behalf of others. He knows that God has blessed him that he might be a blessing to others; and yet, the complaint is generally that believers have no power for this work of bringing blessing to others. They are not, they say, in a condition to exercise an influence over others by their words. This is not to be wondered at, if they will not dwell in the sanctuary. We read that *"The Lord separated the tribe of Levi—to stand before the Lord—and to bless in his name"* (Deuteronomy 10:8). The priestly power of blessing depends on the priestlike life in the presence of God. He who experiences there the power of the blood to preserve him, the helpless one, will have courage to believe that the blood can really deliver others. The holy life-giving power of the blood will create in him the same disposition as that in which Jesus shed it—the sacrifice of himself to redeem others.

In intimacy with God, our love will be set on fire by the love of God; our belief that God will surely make use of us will be strengthened; the Spirit of Jesus will take possession of us to enable us to labor in humility, in wisdom, and in power; and our weakness and poverty will become the vessels in which God's power can work. From our words and examples, blessing will flow because we dwell with Him who is pure blessing; and He will not permit anyone to be near Him without being also filled with His blessing.

Beloved, is not the life prepared for us a glorious and a blessed one: the enjoyment of the blessedness of being near to God; the carrying out of the ministry of His house; the imparting of His blessing to others?

Let no one think that the full blessing is not for him, that such a life is too high for him. In the power of Jesus' blood, we have the assurance that this drawing near is for us also, if only we wholly yield ourselves to it.

For those who truly desire this blessing I give the following advice. Remember that this, and nothing less, is designed for you. All of us who are God's children have been brought nigh by the blood. All of us can desire the full experience of it. Let us only hold this fast: the life of intimacy with God is for me. The Father does not wish that one of His children should be afar off. We cannot please our God as we ought if we live without this blessing. We are priests; grace to live as priests is prepared for us; free entrance into the sanctuary as our abiding place is for us. We can be assured of this: God bestows on us His holy presence for indwelling as our right as His children. Let us lay fast hold of this.

Seek to make the full power of the blood your own possession in all its blessed effects. It is in the power of the blood that relationship is possible. Let your heart be filled with faith in the power of the blood of reconciliation. Sin has been so entirely atoned for and blotted out, that its power to keep you away from God has been completely, and forever, taken away. Live in the joyful profession that sin is powerless to separate you one moment from God. Believe that by the blood you have been fully justified, and thus have a righteous claim to a place in the sanctuary. Let the blood also cleanse you. Expect from the fellowship that follows the inner deliverance from the defilement of sin which still dwells in you. Say with the Scriptures, *"How much more shall the blood of Christ cleanse your conscience to serve the living God."* Let the blood sanctify you, separate you for God in undivided consecration, to be filled by Him. Let the pardoning, cleansing, sanctifying power of the blood have free course in you. You will discover how this brings you, as it were, automatically near to God and protects you.

Do not fear to expect that Jesus Himself will reveal in you the power of the blood to bring you nigh to God. The blood was shed to unite us to God. The blood has accomplished its work, and will perfect it in you. The blood has unspeakable virtue and glory in God's sight.

The mercy seat sprinkled with blood is the chosen place of God's abode and is His throne of grace. He draws near with joy and good pleasure to the heart that surrenders itself entirely to the efficacy of the blood.

The blood has irresistible power. Through the blood Jesus was raised up from the grave and carried into heaven. Be assured the blood is able to preserve you every day in God's presence by its divine life-giving power.

As precious and all powerful as the blood is, so sure and certain is also your abiding with God, if only your trust is steadfast.

"Washed and made white in the blood of the Lamb—therefore are they before the throne of God and serve him day and night in his temple." That word about the eternal glory has a bearing also upon our life on earth. The fuller our faith and experience of the power of the blood, just the closer is the intimacy; the more sure the abiding near the throne, the wider is the entrance to the unbroken ministry of God in His sanctuary; and here on earth, just the greater the power to serve the living God, so the richer the priestly blessing which you will spread around you. O Lord! May this word have its full power over us now, here, and hereafter!

CHAPTER 7

Dwelling in "The Holiest" through the Blood

*"Having therefore, brethren, boldness to enter
into the Holiest by the blood of Jesus,
by a new and living way which he hath
consecrated for us through the veil,
that is to say, his flesh, and having
a great priest over the house of God,
let us draw near with a true heart,
in full assurance of faith,
having our hearts sprinkled
from an evil conscience,
and our bodies washed with pure water."
—Hebrews 10:19-22*

In these words we have a summary of the chief contents of this epistle, and of the good news about God's grace, as the Holy Spirit thus caused it to be presented to the Hebrews and also to us.

Through sin, man was driven out of Eden, away from the presence and fellowship of God. God in His mercy sought from the beginning to restore the broken fellowship.

To this end He gave to Israel, through the shadowy types of the tabernacle, the expectation of a time to come, when the wall of partition should be removed, so that His people might dwell in His presence. *"When shall I come and appear before God"* was the longing sigh of the saints of the Old Covenant.

It is the sigh also of many of God's children under the New Covenant who do not understand that the way into the Holiest has really been opened, and that every child of God may and ought to have his real dwelling place there.

Oh, my brothers and sisters, who long to experience the full power of the redemption which Jesus has accomplished, come with me to hear what our God says to us about the opened Holy Place, and the freedom with which we can enter through the blood.

The passage at the head of this chapter shows us in a first series of four words what God has prepared for us, as the sure ground on which our fellowship with Him may rest. Then in a second series of four words which follow, we learn how we may be prepared to enter into that fellowship and to live in it.

Read the text with attention, and you will see that the words *"let us draw near"* are the center of it all. Let us consider the following:

First, what God has prepared for us;

Second, how God prepares us for what He has prepared for us; and

Finally, *"let us draw near."*

"Having therefore, brethren, boldness to enter into the holiest, by the blood of Jesus, by a new and living way, which he hath consecrated for us, through the veil, that is to say, his flesh, and having a great Priest over the house of God, let us draw near with a true heart, in full assurance of faith, having our hearts cleansed from an evil conscience, and our bodies washed with pure water." (Hebrews 10:19-22)

What God Has Prepared for Us

The Holiest

"Having therefore boldness to enter into 'the holiest' let us draw near."

To bring us into the Holiest is the end of the redemptive work of Jesus, and he who does not know what the Holiest is, cannot enjoy the full benefit of redemption.

What is this Holiest?" It is just the place where God dwells: the Holiest, the dwelling place of the Most High. This does not refer only to heaven, but to the spiritual Holiest place of God's presence.

Under the Old Covenant there was a material sanctuary (Hebrews 8:2, 9:1), the dwelling place of God, in which the priests dwelt in God's presence and served Him. Under the New Covenant there is the true spiritual tabernacle, not confined to any place; the Holiest is where God reveals Himself (John 4:23-25).

What a glorious privilege it is to enter into the Holiest and dwell there, to walk all the day in the presence of God. What a rich blessing is poured out there. In the Holiest the favor and fellowship of God are enjoyed; the life and blessing of God are experienced; the power and joy of God are found. Life is spent in the Holiest in priestly purity and consecration; there the incense of sweet savour is burned and sacrifices acceptable to God are offered. It is a holy life of prayer and blessedness.

Under the Old Covenant, everything was material: the sanctuary also was material and local. Under the New Covenant everything is spiritual: the true Sanctuary owes its existence to the power of the Holy Spirit. Through the

Holy Spirit, a real life in the Holiest is possible, and the knowledge that God walks there can be as certain as in the case of the priests of old. The Spirit makes real in our experience the work Jesus has accomplished.

Believer in Jesus Christ, have you liberty to enter into and abide in the Holiest? As one who has been redeemed, it is a fitting thing for you to make your home there, and not elsewhere, for Christ cannot elsewhere reveal the full power of His redemption. But there, He can bless you richly. Oh! Understand it then, and let the object of God and of our Lord Jesus be yours also. May it be the one desire of our hearts to enter into the Holiest, to live in the Holiest, to minister in the Holiest. We can confidently expect the Holy Spirit to give us a right conception of the glory of entering into a dwelling in the Holiest.

Liberty through the Blood

Admission to the Holiest, like the Holiest itself, belongs to God. God Himself thought of it and prepared it; we have the liberty, the freedom, the right to enter by the blood of Jesus. The blood of Jesus exercises such a wonderful power that through it a son of perdition may obtain full freedom to enter into the divine sanctuary, the Holiest. *"Ye who sometimes were far off are made nigh by the blood of Christ"* (Ephesians 2:13).

And how is it the blood exercises this wonderful power? Scripture says *"the life is in the blood"* (Leviticus 17:11). The power of the blood is in the worth of the life. In the blood of Jesus the power of the divine life dwelt and worked; the blood has already in Him almighty and unceasing power.

But that power could not be exercised for reconciliation until it was first shed. By bearing the punishment of sin unto death, the Lord Jesus conquered the power of sin and brought it to naught. *"The power of sin is the law."* By perfectly fulfilling the law, when He shed His blood under its curse, His blood has made sin entirely powerless. So the blood has its wonderful power, not only because the life of God's Son was in it, but because it was given as an atonement for sin. This is the reason Scripture speaks so highly about the blood. Through the blood of the everlasting covenant, God has brought again from the dead our Lord Jesus (Hebrews 13:20).

Through his own blood He has entered into the Holiest (Hebrews 9:12). The power of the blood has entirely destroyed the power of sin, death, the grave, and hell; so that our surety could go out. The power of the blood has opened heaven so that our surety could freely enter.

And now we also have liberty to enter through the blood. Sin took away our liberty of approach to God; the blood perfectly restores to us this liberty. He who will take time to meditate upon the power of that blood, appropriating it believingly for himself, will obtain a wonderful view of the liberty and directness with which we can now have intimacy with God.

Oh, the divine, wonderful power of the blood! Through the blood, we enter into the Holiest. The blood pleads for us and in us with an eternal, ceaseless effect. It removes sin from God's sight and from our conscience. Every moment we have free, full entrance, and we can have intimacy with God through the blood.

Oh, that the Holy Spirit might reveal to us the full power of the blood! Under His teaching what a full entrance we enjoy to intimate fellowship with the Father. Our life is in the Holiest through the blood.

New and Living Way

"Having therefore, brethren, boldness to enter into the Holiest by the blood of Jesus, by a new and living way, which he hath consecrated for us through the veil, that is to say, his flesh." The blood bestows our right of entrance. The way, as a living and life-giving one, bestows the power. That He has consecrated this

way by His flesh does not mean that this is merely a repetition in other words of the same thought as *"through His blood."* By no means.

Jesus has shed His blood for us; in that particular we cannot follow Him. But the way by which He walked when He shed His blood, the rending of the veil of His flesh, in that way we must follow Him. What He did in the opening of that way is a living power which draws and carries us as we enter the Holiest. The lesson we have to learn here is this—the way into the Holiest is through the rent veil of the flesh.

It was so with Jesus. The veil that separated God and us was the flesh. Sin has its power in the flesh, and only through the taking away of sin, the veil may be removed. When Jesus came in the flesh, He could rend the veil only by dying; and so to bring to nothing the power of the flesh and sin, *"He offered up the flesh, and delivered it to death."* This is what gave to the shedding of His blood its worth and power.

And this remains now the law for each one who desires to enter the Holiest through His blood: it must be through the rent veil of the flesh. The blood demands, the blood accomplishes the rending of the flesh. Where the blood of Jesus works powerfully, there follows, always, the putting to death of the flesh. He who desires to spare the flesh cannot enter into the Holiest. The flesh must be sacrificed, given over to death. In proportion as the believer perceives the sinfulness of his flesh, and puts to death all that is in the flesh, he will better understand the power of the blood. The believer does this, not in his own strength; he comes by a living way which Jesus has consecrated. The life-giving power of Jesus works in this "way." The Christian is crucified and dead with Jesus: *"They that are Christ's have crucified the flesh."* It is in fellowship with Christ that we enter through the veil.

Oh, glorious way, *"the new and living way,"* full of life-giving power, *"which Christ has consecrated for us!"* By this way we have the liberty to enter into the Holiest by the blood of Jesus. May the Lord God lead us along this "way," through the rent veil, through the death of the flesh, to the full life of the Spirit. Then we shall find our dwelling place within the veil, in the Holiest with God. Each sacrifice of the flesh leads us, through the blood, further into the Holiest.

AUTHOR'S NOTE: Compare further, with care, 1 Peter 3:18, *"Christ was put to death in the flesh"*; 4:1, *"Christ hath suffered for us in the flesh, but living in the Spirit"*; and 4:6, *"Condemned sin in the flesh."*

The Great Priest

"And having an high Priest over the house of God, let us draw near."

Praised be God, we have not only the work, but the living person of Christ, as we enter the Holiest; not only the blood and the living way, but Jesus Himself, as *"High Priest over the house of God."*

The priests who went into the earthly sanctuary could do so only because of their relationship to the high priest; none but the sons of Aaron were priests. We have an entrance into the Holiest, because of our relationship to the Lord Jesus. He said to the Father, *"Behold here am I, and the children whom thou hast given me."*

He is the great Priest. The epistle to the Hebrews has shown us that He is the true Melchisedek, the Eternal Son, who has an eternal and changeless priesthood, and as Priest is seated on the throne. He lives there to pray always; therefore also He is able *"to save to the uttermost them that come to God through him,"* a great and all-powerful Priest.

"A High Priest over the house of God," He is appointed over the entire ministry of the Holiest, of the house of God. All the people of God are under His care. If we desire to enter the Holiest, He is there to receive us, and to present us to the Father. He Himself will

complete in us the sprinkling of the blood. Through the blood He has entered, through the blood He brings us also in. He will teach us all the duties of the Holiest and of our responsibilities there. He makes acceptable our prayers, our offerings, and the duties of our ministry, however weak they are. What is more, He bestows on us heavenly light and heavenly power for our work and life in the Holiest. It is He who imparts the life, and the Spirit of the Holiest. Just as His blood procured an entrance, His sacrifice of His flesh is the living way. As we enter, it is He by whom we are kept abiding there, and are able always to walk well pleasing to God. As the sympathetic High Priest, He knows how to stoop to each one, even the weakest. Yes! that is what makes intimacy with God in the Holiest so attractive: we find Jesus there, as a *"High Priest over the house of God."*

And just when it seems to us as if the Holiest is too high or too holy for us, and that we cannot understand what the power of the blood is, and how we are to walk on *"the new and living way,"* just then, we may look up to the living Saviour Himself to teach us and to bring us Himself into the Holiest. He is the Priest over the house of God. You have only to cleave to Him, and you will be in the Holiest.

"Let us draw near," seeing we have the Holiest where God waits for us, and the blood

which gives us liberty, and the living way which carries us, and the High Priest to help us. *"Let us draw near."* Yes, *"let us draw near."* Let nothing hold us back from making use of these wonderful blessings which God has designed for us. It is into the Holiest that we are to enter; our right has been obtained for us by the blood of Jesus; by His own footsteps He has consecrated the way. He lives in His eternal priesthood to receive us in the Holiest, to sanctify, to preserve, to bless us. Oh! Let us not any longer hesitate or turn back. Let us sacrifice all for this one thing; in view of what God has prepared for us, *"let us draw near"* by the hand of Jesus, to appear before our Father, and to find our life in the light of His countenance.

And do we desire to know how we can now be prepared to enter? Our text gives us a glorious answer to this question.

How We Are Prepared

Let Us Draw Near With a True Heart

This is the first of the four demands made on the believer who wishes *"to draw near."* It is coupled with the second demand, *"full assurance of faith,"* and it is chiefly in its union with the second that we understand aright what *"a true heart"* means.

The preaching of the Gospel begins always with repentance and faith. Man cannot receive God's grace by faith if, at the same time, sin is not forsaken. In the progress of the life of faith this law is always binding. The full assurance of faith cannot be reached without *"a true heart,"* a heart that is wholly honest with God, that is surrendered entirely to Him. The Holiest cannot be entered without *"a true heart,"* a heart that is truly desirous of seeking what it professes to seek.

"Let us draw near with a true heart": a heart that truly desires to forsake everything to dwell in the Holiest, and forsaking everything, to possess God; a heart that truly abandons everything in order to yield itself to the authority and power of the blood; a heart that truly chooses *"the new and living way"* in order to go through the veil with Christ by the rending of the flesh; a heart that truly and entirely gives itself to the indwelling and lordship of Jesus.

"Let us draw near with a true heart." Without a true heart there is no entrance into the Holiest.

But who has a true heart? The new heart that God has given is *"a true heart."* Recognize that. By the power of the Spirit of God who dwells in that new heart, place yourself, by an exercise of your will, on the side of God against the sin that is still in your flesh. Say to the

Lord Jesus, the High Priest, that you submit and cast down before Him every sin and all of your self life, forsaking all to follow Him.

And as regards the hidden depths of sin in your flesh, of which you are not yet conscious, and the malice of your heart: for them also provision is made. *"Search me, O God, and know my heart"* (Psalm 139:23). Subject yourself continually to the heart-searching light of the Spirit. He will uncover what is hidden from you. He who does this has a true heart to enter into the Holiest.

Let us not be afraid to say to God that we draw near with a true heart. Let us be assured that God will not judge us according to the perfection of what we do, but according to the honesty with which we yield ourselves to lay aside every known sin, and with which we accept conviction by the Holy Spirit of all our hidden sin. A heart that does this honestly is, in God's sight, a true heart. And with a true heart the Holiest is approached through the blood. Praised be God! Through His Spirit, we have *"a true heart."*

In Full Assurance of Faith

We know what place faith occupies in God's dealings with man. *"Without faith it is impossible to please Him."* Here at the entrance into the Holiest all depends on *"the full assurance of faith."*

There must be *"a full assurance of faith"* that there is a Holy Place where we can dwell and walk with God; that the power of the precious blood has conquered sin so perfectly that nothing can prevent our undisturbed fellowship with God; that the way which Jesus has sanctified through His flesh is a living way, which carries those who tread on it with eternal living power; that the great Priest over the house of God can save to the uttermost those who come to God through Him; and that He by His Spirit works in us everything that is needful for life in the Holiest. These things we must believe and hold fast in *"the full assurance of faith."*

But how can I get there? How can my faith grow to this full assurance? By fellowship with *"Jesus, the author and finisher of our faith"* (Hebrews 12:2). As the great Priest over the house of God, He enables us to appropriate faith. By considering Him, His wonderful love, His perfect work, His precious and all-powerful blood, faith is sustained and strengthened. God has given Him to awaken faith. By keeping our eyes fixed on Him, faith and the full assurance of faith become ours.

In handling the Word of God, remember that *"faith cometh by hearing, and hearing by the Word of God."* Faith comes by the Word and grows by the Word, but not the Word as letter, but as the voice of Jesus; only *"the words that I speak unto you"* are Spirit-life, only in Him are the promises of God *"yea and amen."* Take time to meditate on the Word and treasure it in your heart, but always with a heart set on Jesus Himself. It is faith in Jesus that saves. The Word that is taken to Jesus in prayer and talked over with Him is the Word that is effective.

Remember that *"to him that hath shall be given."* Make use of the faith that you have; exercise it; declare it; and let your believing trust in God become the chief occupation of your life. God wishes to have children who believe Him; He desires nothing so much as faith. Get accustomed to say with each prayer "Lord I believe that I shall obtain this." As you read each promise in Scripture, say, "Lord, I believe You will fulfill this in me." The whole day through, make it your holy habit in everything—yes, in everything—to exercise trust in God's guidance and God's blessing.

To enter into the Holiest, *"full assurance of faith"* is necessary. *"Let us draw near in full assurance of faith."* Redemption through the blood is so perfect and powerful; the love and grace of Jesus so overflowing; the blessedness of dwelling in the Holiest is so surely for us and within our reach—*"Let us draw near in full assurance of faith."*

With Our Heart Cleansed

"Let us draw near...having our hearts sprinkled [cleansed] from an evil conscience."

The heart is the center of human life, and the conscience again is the center of the heart. By his conscience, man realizes his relationship to God; and an evil conscience tells him that all is not right between God and himself, not merely that he commits sin, but that he is sinful, and alienated from God. A good or clear conscience bears witness that he is well pleasing to God (Hebrews 11:5). It bears witness not only that his sins are forgiven but that his heart is sincere before God. He who desires to enter the Holiest must have his heart cleansed from an evil conscience. The words are translated *"our hearts sprinkled from an evil conscience."* It is the sprinkling of the blood that avails. The blood of Christ will purify your conscience to serve the living God.

We have already seen that entrance to the Holiest is by the blood, by which Jesus went into the Father. But that is not enough. There is a twofold sprinkling: the priests who drew near to God were not only reconciled through the sprinkling of blood before God on the altar, but their very persons must be sprinkled with the blood. The blood of Jesus must be so brought by the Holy Spirit into direct contact with our hearts that our hearts become cleansed from an evil conscience. The blood removes all self-condemnation. It cleanses the conscience. Conscience then witnesses that the removal of guilt has been so perfectly completed, there is no longer the least separation between God and us. Conscience bears witness that we are well pleasing to God; that our heart is cleansed; that we through the sprinkling of the blood are in true living fellowship with God. Yes, the blood of Jesus Christ cleanses from all sin, not only from the guilt but also from the stain of sin.

Through the power of the blood, our fallen nature is prevented from exercising its power, just as a fountain by its gentle spray cleanses the grass that otherwise would be covered with dust and keeps it fresh and green, so the blood works with a ceaseless effect to keep the soul clean. A heart that lives under the full power of the blood is a clean heart, cleansed from a guilty conscience, prepared to *"draw near"* with perfect freedom. The whole heart, the whole inner being, is cleansed by a divine operation.

"Let us draw near, having our hearts sprinkled from an evil conscience." Let us *"in full assurance of faith"* believe that our hearts are cleansed. Let us honor the blood greatly, by confessing before God that it cleanses us. The High Priest will, by His Holy Spirit, make us understand the full meaning and power of the words, *"having the heart cleansed by the blood"*;

the entrance to the Holy Place prepared through the blood; and further, our hearts prepared by the blood for entrance. Oh! How glorious then, having the heart cleansed, is it to enter into and to abide in the Holiest.

With the Body Washed

"Let us draw near...having the body washed with pure water."

We belong to two worlds, the seen and the unseen. We have an inner, hidden life that brings us into touch with God; and an outer, bodily life by which we are in relationship with man. If this word refers to the body, it refers to the entire life in the body with all its activities.

The heart must be sprinkled with blood; the body must be washed with pure water. When the priests were consecrated, they were washed with water as well as sprinkled with blood (Exodus 29:4, 20, 21). And if they went into the Holy Place, there was not only the altar with its blood, but also the laver with its water. So also Christ came by water and blood (1 John 5:6). He had His baptism with water and later with blood (Luke 12:50).

There is for us also a twofold cleansing with water and blood. Baptism with water is unto repentance for laying aside of sin. *"Be baptized and wash away your sins."* While the blood cleanses the heart, the inner man, baptism is the yielding of the body, with all its visible life, to separation from sin.

So *"let us draw near, having our hearts cleansed from an evil conscience, and our bodies washed with pure water."* The power of the blood to cleanse inwardly cannot be experienced unless we also cleanse ourselves from all filthiness of the flesh. The divine work of cleansing by the sprinkling of blood and the human work of cleansing by laying aside sin are inseparable.

We must be clean to enter into the Holiest. Just as you would never dream of entering in to the presence of a king unwashed, so you cannot imagine that you could come into the presence of God, in the Holy Place, if you are not cleansed from every sin. In the blood of Christ that cleanses from all sin, God has bestowed on you the power to cleanse yourself. Your desire to live with God in the Holiest must always be united with the most careful laying aside of even the least sin. The unclean may not enter the Holiest.

Praised be God, He desires to have us there. As His priests, we must minister to Him there. He desires our purity that we may enjoy the blessing of the Holiest—that is, His holy fellowship. And He has taken care that through the blood and by the Spirit, we may be clean.

"Let us draw near, having our heart sprinkled, and the body washed with pure water."

"Let Us Draw Near"

The Holiest Place is open even for those in our congregations who have not yet truly turned to the Lord. For them also the sanctuary has been opened. The precious blood, the living way, and the High Priest are for them also. With great confidence we dare to invite even them, *"Let us draw near."* Oh! Despise not, my friends still far from God; oh, despise no longer God's wonderful grace; draw near to the Father who has so earnestly sent this invitation to you, who at the cost of the blood of His Son has opened a way for you into the Holiest, who waits in love to receive you again into His dwelling place as His child. Oh! I beseech you, *"let us [all] draw near."* Jesus Christ, the High Priest over the House of God, is a perfect Savior.

"Let us draw near." The invitation comes especially to all believers. Be not satisfied to stand in the porch. It is not sufficient to cherish the hope that your sins are forgiven. *"Let us draw near"*; let us enter within the veil; let us in spirit press on to real nearness to our God. *"Let us draw near"* and live nearer to God,

wholly take our abode in His holy presence. *"Let us draw near"*; our place is the innermost sanctuary.

"Let us draw near with a true heart in full assurance of faith." He who gives himself sincerely and entirely to God will through the Holy Spirit experience *"the full assurance of faith"* to take for himself, freely and gladly, all that the Word has promised. Our weakness of faith arises from duplicity of heart. *"Let us draw near with a true heart in full assurance"* that the blessing is ours. The blood has so perfectly atoned for and conquered sin that nothing can hold the believer back from free admission to God.

"Let us draw near, having our hearts sprinkled from an evil conscience and our bodies washed with pure water." Let us receive into our hearts faith in the perfect power of the blood, and let us lay aside everything that is not in accord with the purity of the Holy Place. Then we begin to feel ourselves daily more at home in the Holiest. In Christ, who is our Life, we are also there. Then we learn to carry on all our work in the Holiest. All that we do is a spiritual sacrifice well pleasing to God in Jesus Christ. Brethren, *"let us draw near"* as God waits for us in the Holiest.

"Let us draw near." That call has special reference to prayer. Not as though we, as priests, are not always in the Holiest, but there

are moments of closer fellowship when the soul turns itself entirely to God to be engaged with Him alone. Alas! Our prayer is too often a calling out to God from a distance, with little power in it. Let us with each prayer see that we are really in the Holiest. Let us with hearts perfectly sprinkled from an evil conscience, in silent faith, appropriate the full effect of the blood, by which sin, as a separation between God and us, is entirely removed. Let us take time till we know that now, "I am in the Holiest through the blood," and then pray. Then we can lay our desires and wishes before our Father in the assurance that they are acceptable incense. Then prayer is a true *"drawing near"* to God, an exercise of inner fellowship with Him; then we have courage and power to carry on our work of priestly intercession and to pray blessings on others. He who dwells in the Holy Place through the power of the blood is truly one of God's saints, and the power of God's holy and blessed presence goes out from him upon those who are round about him.

Brethren, *"let us draw near."* Let us pray for ourselves, for one another, for everyone. Let the Holiest so become our fixed abode that we may carry about with us everywhere the presence of our God. Let this be the fountain of life for us that grows from strength to strength, from glory to glory, always dwelling in the Holiest by the blood. Amen.

CHAPTER 8

Life in the Blood

*"Jesus said unto them, Verily, verily,
I say unto you, Except ye eat the flesh of the
Son of Man, and drink his blood,
ye have no life in you.
Whoso eateth my flesh, and drinketh my
blood, hath eternal life;
and I will raise him up at the last day.
For my flesh is meat indeed,
and my blood is drink indeed.
He that eateth my flesh, and drinketh
my blood dwelleth in me and I in him."*
—*John 6:53-56*

*"The cup of blessing which we bless, is it not
the communion of the blood of Christ?"*
—*1 Corinthians 10:16*

The drinking of the blood of the Lord Jesus is
the subject brought before us in these words.
Just as water has a twofold effect, so is it also
with this holy blood.

When water is used for washing, it cleanses; but if we drink it, we are refreshed and revived. He who desires to know the full power of the blood of Jesus must be taught by Him what the blessing of drinking the blood is. Everyone knows the difference there is between washing and drinking. Necessary and pleasant as it is to use water for cleansing, it is much more necessary and reviving to drink it. Without its cleansing, it is not possible to live as we ought; but without drinking, we cannot live at all. It is only by drinking that we enjoy the full benefit of its power to sustain life.

Without drinking the blood of the Son of God—that is, without the most hearty appropriation of it—eternal life cannot be obtained.

To many there is something unpleasant in the phrase "drinking the blood of the Son of Man," but it was still more disagreeable to the Jews, for the use of blood was forbidden by the law of Moses under severe penalties. When Jesus spoke of "drinking His blood," it naturally annoyed them—but it was an unspeakable offense to their religious feelings. Our Lord, we may be sure, would not have used the phrase had He been able otherwise to make plain to them and to us the deepest and most glorious truths concerning salvation by the blood.

In seeking to become partakers of the salvation here spoken of as "drinking the blood of our Lord," let us endeavor to understand the following:

First, what the blessing is which is described as "drinking the blood";

Second, how this blessing is wrought out in us; and

Last, what should be our attitude towards it.

The Blessing of "Drinking the Blood"

We saw just now that drinking expresses a much more intimate connection with water than washing, and hence produces a more powerful effect. There is a blessing in the fellowship with the blood of Jesus which goes much farther than cleansing or sanctification; rather, we are enabled to see how far reaching is the influence of the blessing indicated by this phrase.

Not only must the blood do something for us, by placing us in a new relationship to God; but it must do something in us, entirely renewing us within. It is to this that the words of the Lord Jesus draw our attention when He says: *"Unless ye eat the flesh of the Son of man, and*

drink his blood, ye have no life in you." Our
Lord distinguishes two kinds of life. The Jews
there in His presence had a natural life of body
and soul. Many among them were devout,
well-intentioned men, but He said they had no
life in them unless they *"ate his flesh and
drank his blood."* They needed another life—a
new, heavenly life which He possessed and
which He could impart. All creature life must
obtain nourishment outside of itself. The natural life was naturally nourished by bread and
water. The heavenly life must be nourished by
heavenly food and drink by Jesus Himself.
*"Except ye eat the flesh of the Son of man, and
drink his blood, ye have no life in you."* Nothing
less must become ours than His life—the life
that He, as Son of man, lived on earth.

Our Lord emphasized this still more
strongly in words which follow, in which He
again explained what the nature of that life is:
*"Whoso eateth my flesh and drinketh my blood
hath eternal life and I will raise him up at the
last day."* Eternal life is the life of God. Our
Lord came to earth in the first place to reveal
that eternal life in the flesh and then to com-
municate it to us who are in the flesh. In Him
we see the eternal life dwelling in its divine
power, in a body of flesh, which was taken up
into heaven. He tells us that those who eat His
flesh and drink His blood, who partake of His
body as their sustenance, will experience also

in their own bodies the power of eternal life. *"I will raise him up at the last day."* The marvel of the eternal life in Christ is that it was eternal life in a human body. We must be partakers of that body, not less than in the activities of His Spirit; then our body, also possessing that life, will one day be raised from the dead.

Our Lord said, *"My flesh is meat indeed and my blood is drink indeed."* The word translated *indeed* here is the same as that He used when He spoke His parable of the true vine: *"I am the true [the indeed] vine,"* thus indicating the difference between what was only a symbol and what is actual truth. Earthly food is no real food, for it imparts no real life. The one true food is the body and blood of the Lord Jesus Christ which imparts and sustains life, and that in no shadowy or merely symbolical manner. No, this word so frequently repeated, indicates that in a full and real sense the flesh and blood of the Lord Jesus are the food by which eternal life is nourished and sustained in us: *"My flesh is meat indeed, and my blood is drink indeed."*

In order to point out the reality and power of this food our Lord added, *"He that eateth my flesh and drinketh my blood dwelleth in me and I in him."* Nourishment by His flesh and blood effects the most perfect union with Him. This is the reason that His flesh and blood have such power of eternal life. Our Lord declares here that those who believe in Him are to experience not only certain influences from Him in their hearts, but are to be brought into the most close and abiding union with Him. *"He that drinketh my blood dwelleth in me and I in him."*

This then is the blessing of drinking the blood of the Son of man: becoming one with Him, becoming a partaker of the divine nature in Him. How real this union is may be seen from the words which follow: *"As I live by the Father, so he that eateth me even he shall live by me."* Nothing save the union which exists between our Lord and the Father can serve as a type of our union with Him. Just as in the indivisible, divine nature, the two Persons are truly One, so man becomes one with Jesus; the union is just as real as that in the divine nature, only with this difference—that as human nature cannot exist apart from the body, this union includes the body also.

Our Lord *"prepared for himself"* a body into which He took up a human body. This body became, by the body and blood of Jesus, a sharer in eternal life, in the life of our Lord Himself. Those who desire to receive the fullness of this blessing must be careful to enjoy all that the Scripture offers them in the holy mysterious expression "to drink the blood of Christ."

How This Blessing Is
Worked Out in Us

We shall now try to understand what the "drinking of the blood of Jesus" really is.

The first idea that here presents itself is that "drinking" indicates the deep, true appropriation in our spirit, by faith, of all we understand concerning the power of the blood.

We speak sometimes of "drinking in" the words of a speaker when we heartily give ourselves up to listen and receive them. So when the heart of anyone is filled with a sense of the preciousness and power of the blood, when he with real joy is lost in the contemplation of it, when he with whole-hearted faith takes it for himself and seeks to be convinced in his inner being of the life-giving power of that blood, then it may be rightly said that he "drinks the blood of Jesus." All that faith enables him to see of redemption, of cleansing, of sanctification by the blood, he absorbs into the depths of his soul.

There is a deep truth in this representation, and it gives us a very glorious demonstration of the way in which the full blessing by the blood may be obtained. And yet it is certain that our Lord intended something more than this by so repeatedly making use of the expression about *eating his flesh and drinking his blood.* What this further truth is becomes

137

clear by his institution of the Lord's Supper. For, although our Saviour did not actually deal with that Supper when He taught in Capernaum, yet He spoke on the subject of which later on the Supper was made the visible confirmation.

In the Reformed churches there are two aspects of viewing the Holy Supper. According to one which is called after the name of the Reformer Zwingli, the bread and wine in the Supper are merely tokens, or representations of a spiritual truth, to teach us that just as, and as sure as, bread and wine when eaten or drunk, nourish and revive, so surely—and even more surely—the body and blood recognized and appropriated by faith nourish and quicken the soul.

According to the other view which bears the name of Calvin, there is something more than this in the eating of the Supper. He teaches that in a hidden and incomprehensible way, but yet really, we, through the Holy Spirit, become so nourished by the body and blood of Jesus in heaven, that even our bodies, through the power of His body, become partakers in the power of eternal life. Hence He connects the resurrection of the body with the eating of Christ's body in the Supper. He writes thus:

"The bodily presence which the Sacrament demands is such, and exercises such a power here (in the Supper) that it becomes not only the undoubted assurance in our spirit of eternal life, but also assures the immortality of the flesh. If anyone asks me how this can be, I am not ashamed to acknowledge that it is a mystery too high for my spirit to comprehend, or my words to express. I feel it more than I can understand it.

"It may seem incredible indeed that the flesh of Christ should reach us from such immense local distance so as to become our food. But we must remember how far the power of the Holy Spirit transcends all our senses. Let faith then embrace what the understanding cannot grasp, namely: the sacred communication of His flesh and blood by which Christ transfuses His life into us, just as if it penetrated our bones and marrow."

The communion of the flesh and blood of Christ is necessary for all who desire to inherit eternal life. The apostle Paul says, *"The Church...is his body"* (Ephesians 1:23); *"He is the head from whom the whole body fitly joined together maketh increase of the body"* (Ephesians 4:15, 16). Our bodies are *"members of Christ"* (1 Corinthians 6:15-16). We see that all this cannot take place if He is not attached to us in body and spirit. The apostle again makes use of a glorious expression, *"We are members of his body, of his flesh and of his bones."* Then he cries out, *"The mystery is great."* It would therefore be folly not to recognize the communion of believers in the body and blood of the Lord, a communion which the apostle esteemed so great that he wondered at it rather than explained it.

There is something more in the Supper than simply the believer appropriating the redemptive work of Christ. This is made clear in the Heidelberg catechism in Question 76: "What is it then to eat the crucified body of Christ and to drink His shed blood?" The answer is, "It is not only to embrace with a believing heart all the sufferings and death of Christ, and thereby to receive pardon of sin and eternal life; but, also, besides that, to become more and more united to His sacred body, by the Holy Spirit who dwells at once both in Christ and in us, so that we, though Christ is in heaven and we on earth, are, notwithstanding, flesh of His flesh, and bone of His bones; and we live and are governed for ever by one Spirit." The thoughts that are expressed in this teaching are in entire agreement with Scripture.

In the creation of man, the remarkable thing which should distinguish him from the spirits which God had previously created, and which should make man the crowning work of God's wisdom and power was that he should reveal the life of the spirit and the glory of God in a body formed out of dust. Through the body, lust and sin came into the world. Full redemption is designed to deliver the body and to make it God's abode. Redemption will be perfect and God's purpose accomplished only then. This was the purpose for which the Lord Jesus came in the flesh, and in Him dwelt *"all the fullness of the Godhead bodily."* For this He bore our sins in His body on the tree; and by His death and resurrection, He delivered the body, as well as the spirit, from the power of sin and death.

As the first fruits of this redemption, we are now one body, as well as one Spirit, with Him. We are of His body, of His flesh, and of His bones. It is because of this that, in the observance of the Holy Supper, the Lord comes to the body also and takes possession of it. Not only does He work by His Spirit on our spirit, so as to make our body share in redemption at the resurrection. No, already here, the body is the temple of the Spirit; and the sanctification of soul and spirit will progress the more gloriously, just in proportion as the undivided personality, including the body, which exercises such an opposing influence, has a share in it.

Thus we are in the Supper so intentionally fed by "the real natural body, and the real blood of Christ"[1]—not following the teaching of Luther that the body of Christ is so in the bread that even an unbeliever eats the holy body—but in such wise "real," that faith, in a secret way, by the Spirit, really receives the power of the holy body and blood from heaven as the food by which soul and body become partakers of eternal life.

All that has now been said about the Supper must have its full application to "the drinking of the blood of Jesus." It is a deep spiritual mystery in which the most intimate, the most perfect union with Christ, is effected. It takes place where the soul, through the Holy Spirit, fully appropriates the communion of the blood of Christ, and becomes a true partaker of the very disposition which He revealed in the shedding of His blood. The blood is the soul, the life of the body; where the believer as one body with Christ desires to abide perfectly in Him, there through the Spirit in a superhuman powerful way, the blood will support and strengthen the heavenly life. The life that was poured out in the blood becomes his life. The life of the old "I" dies to make room for the life of Christ in him. By perceiving how this drinking is the highest participation in the heavenly life of the Lord, faith has one of its highest and most glorious offices.

Our Attitude toward This Drinking

Beloved brethren, you have already heard that we have here one of the deepest mysteries of the life of God in us. It behooves us to draw near with very deep reverence while we ask the Lord Jesus to teach us and bestow upon us what He means by this "drinking of His blood."

Only he who longs for full union with Jesus will learn aright what it is to drink the blood of Jesus. *"He that drinketh my blood dwelleth in me and I in him."* He who is satisfied with just the forgiveness of his sins; he who does not thirst to be made to drink abundantly of the love of Jesus; he who does not desire to experience redemption for soul and body, in its full power, so as to have truly in himself the same disposition that was in Jesus—he will have but a small share in this "drinking of the blood." On the other hand, he who sets before him as his chief object that which is also the object of Jesus—*"abide in me and I in you"*—and who desires that the power of eternal life should operate in his body, he will not suffer himself to be frightened by the impression that these words are too high or too mysterious. He longs to become heavenly-minded because he belongs to heaven and is going there; therefore, he desires to obtain his meat and drink also from heaven. Without thirst, there is no drinking. The longing after Jesus and perfect fellowship with Him is the thirst which is the best preparation for being made to drink the blood.

It is by the Holy Spirit that the thirsty soul will be made to drink of the heavenly refreshment of this life-giving drink. We have already said that this drinking is a heavenly mystery. In heaven where God, the Judge of all is, and where Jesus, the Mediator of the New Covenant is, there also is *the blood of sprinkling*" (Hebrews 12:23, 24). When the Holy Spirit teaches us—taking us, as it were, by the hand—He bestows more than our merely human understanding can grasp. All the thoughts that we can entertain about the blood or the life of Jesus, about our share in that blood as members of His body, and about the impartation to us of the living power of that blood, all are but feeble rays of the glorious reality which He, the Holy Spirit, will bring into being in us through our union with Jesus.

Where, I pray, in our human bodies, do we find that the blood is actually received and, as it were, drunk in? Is it not where one member of the body after another, through the veins, receives the bloodstream which is continually renewed from the heart? Each member of a healthy body ceaselessly and abundantly drinks in the blood. So the Spirit of Life in Christ Jesus, who unites us to Him, will make this drinking of the blood the natural action of the inner life. When the Jews complained that what the Lord had spoken concerning eating His flesh and drinking His blood was *"a hard saying,"* He said, *"It is the Spirit that quickeneth, the flesh profiteth nothing."* It is the Holy Spirit who makes this divine mystery life and power in us—a true living experience, in which we abide in Jesus and He in us.

There must be on our part a quiet, strong, settled expectancy of faith that this blessing will be bestowed on us. We must believe that all the precious blood can do or bestow is really for us.

Let us believe that the Saviour Himself will cause us, through the Holy Spirit, to drink His blood unto life. Let us believe, and very heartily and continuously appropriate, those effects of the blood which we understand better: namely, its reconciling, cleansing, sanctifying effects.

We may then with the greatest certainty and joy, say to the Lord: "O Lord, Your blood is my life-drink. You who have washed and cleansed me by that blood, You will teach me every day *'to eat the flesh of the Son of man, and to drink His blood'* so that I may abide in You and You in me." He will surely do this.

Chapter Note

[1] The words within quotation marks, "the real natural body and the real blood of Christ," are quoted by Dr. Murray from the Articles of the Confession of Faith of the Reformed Churches of Holland, but Dr. Murray did not add the words immediately following which declare that "the manner of our partaking of the same is not by the mouth, but by the Spirit, through faith." Dr. Murray remained true to the Reformed faith. His own view is expressed on page 140 by the words quoted by the Heidelberg Catechism.

CHAPTER 9

Victory through the Blood

"They overcame him by the blood of the Lamb,
and by the word of their testimony; and
they loved not their lives unto death."
—*Revelation 12:11*

For thousands of years there had been a mighty conflict for the possession of mankind, between the old serpent, who led man astray, and *"the seed of the woman."* Often it seemed as though the kingdom of God had come in power; then at other times the might of evil obtained such supremacy that the strife appeared to be hopeless.

It was thus also in the life of our Lord Jesus. By His coming and His wonderful words and works, the most glorious expectations of a speedy redemption were awakened. How terrible was the disappointment which the death of Jesus brought to all who had believed in Him! It seemed, indeed, as if the powers of darkness had conquered and had established their kingdom forever.

But, behold! Jesus is risen from the dead; an apparent victory proved to be the terrible downfall of the prince of darkness. By bringing about the death of *"the Lord of life,"* Satan permitted Him, who alone was able to break open the gates of death, to enter his kingdom. *"Through death he has destroyed him that had the power of death, that is the devil."* In that holy moment when our Lord shed His blood in death, and it seemed as if Satan were victorious, the adversary was robbed of the authority he had hitherto possessed.

Our text gives a very grand representation of these memorable events. The best commentators, notwithstanding differences in details of exposition, are united in thinking that we have here a vision of the casting out of Satan from heaven as a result of the ascension of Christ.

We read in Revelation 12:5-9:

> *And she brought forth a man child, who...was caught up unto God, and to his throne...And there was war in heaven; and Michael and his angels fought against the dragon; and the dragon fought, and his angels, and prevailed not; neither was their place found any more in heaven. And the dragon was cast out, that old serpent, called the Devil, and Satan, which deceiveth the*

whole world: he was cast out into the earth, and his angels were cast out with him.

Then follows the song from which the text is taken:

"Now is come salvation, and strength, and the kingdom of our God, and the power of his Christ, for the accuser of our brethren is cast down, which accused them before our God day and night. And they overcame him by the blood of the Lamb, and by the word of their testimony; and they loved not their lives even unto death. Therefore rejoice, ye heavens, and ye that dwell therein."
(Revelation 12:10-11)

The point which deserves our special attention is that, while the conquest of Satan and his being cast out of heaven, is first represented as the result of the ascension of Jesus and the war in heaven which followed, yet in the song of triumph which was heard in heaven, victory is ascribed chiefly to the blood of the Lamb; this was the power by which the victory was gained.

Through the whole book of Revelation, we see the Lamb on the throne. It is as the slain Lamb that He has gained that position: the victory over Satan and all his authority is by the blood of the Lamb.

We have spoken about the blood in its manifold effects; it is fitting that we should seek to understand how it is that victory is always ascribed to the blood of the Lamb. We shall consider:

First, victory as gained once for all;

Second, victory as being ever carried on; and

Third, victory as one in which we have a share.

The Victory Which Was Gained Once for All

In the exalted representation given in our text, we see what a high position was once occupied by Satan, the great enemy of the human race. He had entrance into heaven and appeared there as the accuser of the brethren and as the opponent of whatever was done in the interests of God's people.

We know how this is taught in the Old Testament. In the book of Job, we see Satan coming with the Sons of God to present himself before the Lord and to obtain permission from

Him to tempt His servant Job (Job 2). In the book of Zechariah, we read that he saw *"Joshua the High Priest standing before the angel of the Lord, and Satan standing at his right hand to resist him [or, be his adversary (RV)]"* (3:1-2). Then there is the statement of our Lord, recorded in Luke 10:18, *"I beheld Satan as lightning fall from heaven."* Later on, in His agony of soul, as He felt beforehand His approaching sufferings, He said, *"Now is the judgment of this world, now shall the prince of this world be cast out"* (John 12:31).

It may, at first thought, seem strange that the Scriptures should represent Satan as being in heaven. But to understand this aright, it is necessary to remember that heaven is not a small, circumscribed dwelling place where God and Satan had relationship as neighbors. No! Heaven is an limitless sphere, with very many different divisions, filled with innumerable hosts of angels who carry out God's will in nature. Among them, Satan also still held a place. Then remember, he is not represented in Scripture to be the black, grisly figure in outward appearance as he is generally pictured, but as *"an angel of light."* He was a prince with ten thousands of servants.

When he had brought about the fall of man, and had also transferred the world to himself and became its prince, he had real authority over all that was in it. Man had been destined to be king of this world, for God has said, *"Have thou authority."* When Satan had conquered the king, he took his entire kingdom under his authority; and this authority was recognized by God. God, in His holy will, had ordained that if man listened to Satan, he must suffer the consequences and become subject to his tyranny. God never in this matter used His power or exercised force, but always took the way of law and right; and so Satan retained his authority until it was taken from him in a lawful manner.

This is the reason why he could appear before God in heaven, as accuser of the brethren and in opposition to them for the 4,000 years of the Old Covenant. He had obtained authority over all flesh, and only after he was conquered in flesh, as the sphere of his authority, could he be cast out forever, as accuser, from the court of heaven.

So the Son of God also had to come in the flesh, in order to fight and conquer Satan, on his own ground.

For this reason also at the commencement of His public life, our Lord, after His anointing, being thus openly recognized as the Son of God, *"was led by the Spirit into the wilderness to be tempted of the devil."* Victory over Satan could be gained only after He had personally endured and resisted his temptations.

But even this victory was not sufficient. Christ came in order that *"through death he might destroy him that had the power of death, that is the devil."* The devil had that power of death because of the law of God. That law had installed him as jailer of its prisoners. Scripture says, *"The sting of death is sin, and the power of sin is the law."* Victory over and the casting out of Satan could not take place till the righteous demands of the law were perfectly fulfilled. The sinner must be delivered from the power of the law, before he could be delivered from the authority of Satan.

It was through His death and the shedding of His blood that the Lord Jesus fulfilled the law's demands. Ceaselessly, the law had been declaring that *"the wages of sin is death,"* and *"the soul that sinneth it shall die."* By the typical ministry of the temple, by the sacrifices with the shedding of blood and sprinkling of blood, the law had foretold that reconciliation and redemption could take place only by the shedding of blood. As our surety, the Son of God was born under the law. He obeyed it perfectly. He resisted the temptations of Satan to withdraw Himself from under its authority. He willingly gave Himself up to bear the punishment of sin. He gave no ear to the temptation of Satan to refuse the cup of suffering. When He shed His blood, He had devoted His whole life, to its very end, to the fulfilling of the law. When the law had been thus perfectly fulfilled, the authority of sin and Satan was brought to an end. Therefore death could not hold Him. *"Through the blood of the everlasting covenant"* God brought Him *"again from the dead."* So also He *"entered heaven by his own blood"* to make His reconciliation effective for us.

The text gives us a striking description of the glorious result of the appearing of our Lord in heaven. We read concerning the mystic woman:

> *She brought forth a man-child, who was to rule all nations with a rod of iron, and her child was caught up unto God, and to his throne...There was war in heaven: Michael and his angels fought against the dragon; and the dragon fought, and his angels, and prevailed not, neither was their place found any more in heaven. And the great dragon was cast out, that old serpent, called the Devil, and Satan, which deceiveth the whole world: and he was cast out into the earth, and his angels were cast out with him."*
> *(Revelation 12:5, 7-9)*

Then follows the song of victory in which the words of our text occur: *"They overcame him by the blood of the Lamb."*

154

In the book of Daniel we read of a previous conflict between this Michael, who stood on the side of God's people Israel, and the opposing world powers. But only now can Satan be cast out, because of the blood of the Lamb. Reconciliation for sin and the fulfillment of the law have taken from him all his authority and right. The blood, as we have already seen, that had done such wonderful things in heaven with God in blotting out sin and bringing it to naught, had a similar power over Satan. He has now no longer any right to accuse. *"Now is come salvation, and strength, and the kingdom of our God, and the power of his Christ, for the accuser of our brethren is cast down...And they overcame him by the blood of the Lamb."*

Victory As Being Ever Carried On

There is a progressive victory which follows on this first victory. Satan having been cast down to earth, the heavenly victory must now be carried out here. This is indicated in the words of the song of victory, *"They overcame him by the blood of the Lamb."* This was primarily spoken concerning *"the brethren"* mentioned, but it refers also to the victory of the angels. The victory in heaven and on earth progresses simultaneously, resting on the same ground. We know from the portion in Daniel already mentioned (Daniel 10:12-13) what fellowship there exists between heaven and earth in carrying on the work of God. As soon as Daniel prayed, the angel became active, and the three weeks' strife in the heavenlies were three weeks of prayer and fasting on earth. The conflict here on earth is the result of a conflict in the invisible region of the heavenlies. Michael and his angels, as well as the brethren on earth, gained the victory *"by the blood of the Lamb."*

In the twelfth chapter of Revelation we are clearly taught how the conflict was removed from heaven to earth. *"Woe to the inhabitants of the earth"* exclaimed the voice in heaven, *"for the devil is come down unto you, having great wrath, because he knoweth that he hath but a short time...And when the dragon saw that he was cast down unto the earth, he persecuted the woman which brought forth the man-child."* The woman signifies nothing else than the church of God, out of which Jesus was born: when the devil could not harm Him any more, he persecutes His church. The disciples of our Lord and the church in the first three centuries had experience of this. In the bloody persecutions in which hundreds of thousands of Christians perished as martyrs, Satan did his utmost to lead the church into apostasy or to root it out altogether; but in its full sense, the statement that *"they overcame by the blood of the Lamb, and by the word of their testimony; and they loved not their lives even unto death*" applies to the martyrs.

After the centuries of persecution, there came to the church centuries of rest and worldly prosperity. Satan had tried force in vain. By the favor of the world, he might have better success. In the church conformed to the world, everything became darker and darker, till in the Middle Ages the Romish apostasy reached its climax. Nevertheless during all these ages there were not a few who in the midst of surrounding misery fought the fight of faith, and by the piety of their lives and witness for the Lord, the statement was often established: *"they overcame him by the blood of the Lamb and by the word of their testimony, and they loved not their lives even unto death."*

This was no less the secret power by which, through the blessed Reformation, the mighty authority which Satan had gained in the church was broken down. *"They overcame him by the blood of the Lamb."* It was the discovery, and experience, and preaching of the glorious truth that we are *"justified freely by his grace, through the redemption that is in Christ Jesus, whom God hath set forth to be a propitiation through faith in his blood,"* that gave to the Reformers such wonderful power and such a glorious victory.

Since the days of the Reformation, it is still apparent that in proportion as the blood of the Lamb is gloried in, the church is constantly inspired by a new life to obtain the victory over deadness or error. Yes, even in the midst of the wildest heathen, where the throne of Satan has been undisturbed for thousands of years, this is still the weapon by which its power must be destroyed. The preaching of *the blood of the cross* as the reconciliation for the sin of the world and the ground of God's free, forgiving love is the power by which the most darkened heart is opened and softened, and, from being a dwelling place of Satan, is changed into a temple of the Most High.

What avails for the church is available also for each Christian. In *the blood of the Lamb,* he always has victory. It is when the soul is convinced of the power which that blood has with God in heaven to effect a perfect reconciliation by the blotting out of sin; to rob the devil of his authority over us completely and for ever; to work out in our hearts a full assurance of the favor of God; and to destroy the power of sin—it is, I say, when the soul lives in the power of the blood that the temptations of Satan cease to ensnare.

Where the holy blood of the Lamb is sprinkled, there God dwells, and Satan is put to flight. In heaven, on earth, and in our hearts, that word as the announcement of a progressive victory is valid: *"they overcame him by the blood of the Lamb."*

Our Share in This Victory

We also have a share in this victory if we are reckoned among those who have been cleansed *"by the blood of the Lamb."* To have the full enjoyment of this, we must pay attention to the following facts.

No Victory without Conflict

We must recognize that we dwell in an enemy's territory. What was revealed to the apostle in his heavenly vision must hold good in our daily lives. Satan has been cast down into the earth; he has great wrath because he has but a short time. He cannot now reach the glorified Jesus, but seeks to reach Him by attacking His people. We must live always under the holy consciousness that we are watched, every moment, by an enemy of unimaginable cunning and power who is unwearied in his endeavor to bring us entirely, or even partially—however little it may be— under his authority. He is literally *"the prince of this world."* All that is in the world is ready to serve him, and he knows how to make use of it in his attempts to lead the church to be unfaithful to her Lord, and to inspire her with his spirit, the spirit of the world.

He makes use not only of temptations to what is commonly esteemed to be sin, but he knows how to gain an entrance into our earthly engagements and businesses—in the seeking for our daily bread and necessary money, in our politics, in our commercial combinations, in our literature and science, in our knowledge, and all things—so to make all that is lawful in itself into a tool to forward his devilish deceptions.

The believer who desires to share in the victory over Satan *"through the blood of the Lamb"* must be a fighter. He must take pains to understand the character of his enemy. He must allow himself to be taught by the Spirit through the Word what the secret cunning of Satan is, which is called in Scripture *"the depths of Satan,"* by which he so often blinds and deceives men. He must know that this strife is *"not against flesh and blood, but against principalities, against powers, against the rulers of the darkness of this world, against spiritual wickedness in high places"* (Ephesians 6:12). He must devote himself, in every way, and at all costs, to carry on the strife till death. Then only will he be able to join in the song of victory, *"They overcame him by the blood of the*

Lamb, and by the word of their testimony; and they loved not their lives even unto death."

Victory through Faith

"This is the victory that overcometh the world, even our faith. Who is he that overcometh the world but he that believeth that Jesus is the Son of God?" (1 John 5:4-5). *"Be of good cheer,"* said our Lord Jesus, *"I have overcome the world."* Satan is an already conquered enemy. He has nothing, absolutely nothing by right, to say to one who belongs to the Lord Jesus. By unbelief, by ignorance of, or by letting go my hold of the fact that I have a participation in the victory of Jesus, I may give Satan again an authority over me which otherwise he does not possess. But when I know, by a living faith, that I am one with the Lord Jesus, that the Lord Himself lives in me, and that He maintains and carries on in me that victory which He gained, then Satan has no power over me. Victory *"through the blood of the Lamb"* is the power of my life.

Only this faith can inspire courage and joy in the strife. By thinking of the terrible power of the enemy, of his never-sleeping watchfulness, of the way in which he has taken possession of everything on earth by which to tempt us, it might well be said—as some Christians

161

think—that the strife is too severe, that it is not possible to live always under such tension, that life would be impossible. This is perfectly true, if we in our weakness had to meet the enemy or gain the victory by our own might. But that is not what we are called upon to do. Jesus is the victor; so we need only to have our souls filled with the heavenly vision of Satan being cast out of heaven by Jesus, filled with faith in the blood by which Jesus Himself conquered, and filled with faith that He Himself is with us to maintain the power and victory of His blood. Then we also *are more than conquerors through him that loved us.*

Victory in Fellowship with the Blood of the Lamb

Faith is not merely a thought of which I lay hold, a conviction that possesses me—it is a life. Faith brings the soul into direct contact with God and the unseen things of heaven, but above all, with the blood of Jesus. It is not possible to believe in victory over Satan by the blood without being myself brought entirely under its power.

Belief in the power of the blood awakens in me a desire for an experience of its power in myself; each experience of its power makes belief in victory more glorious.

Seek to enter more deeply into the perfect reconciliation with God which is yours. Live, constantly, exercising faith in the assurance that *"the blood cleanseth from all sin"*; yield yourself to be sanctified and brought nigh to God through the blood; let it be your life-giving nourishment and power. You will thus have an unbroken experience of victory over Satan and his temptations. He who, as a consecrated priest, walks with God, will rule as a conquering king of Satan.

Believers, our Lord Jesus by His blood has made us not only priests but kings unto God, that we may draw near to God not only in priestly purity and ministry, but that also in kingly power we may rule for God. A kingly spirit must inspire us, a kingly courage to rule over our enemies. The blood of the Lamb must increasingly be a token and seal, not only of reconciliation for all guilt, but of victory over all the power of sin.

The resurrection and ascension of Jesus and the casting out of Satan were the results of the shedding of His blood. In you also, the sprinkling of the blood will open the way for the full enjoyment of resurrection with Jesus, and of being seated with Him in the heavenly places.

I once more, therefore, beseech you to open your entire being to the incoming of the power of the blood of Jesus. Your life will become a continual observance of the resurrection and ascension of our Lord and a continual victory over all the powers of hell. Your heart, too, will constantly unite with the song of heaven, *"Now is come salvation, and strength, and the kingdom of our God, and the power of his Christ, for the accuser of the brethren is cast down. They overcame him by the blood of the Lamb"* (Revelation 12:10-11).

CHAPTER 10

Heavenly Joy through the Blood

*"After this I beheld, and lo, a great multitude,
which no man could number...which stood
before the throne, and before the Lamb...
and they cried with a loud voice saying,
'Salvation to our God which sitteth upon
the throne, and unto the Lamb.'
These are they which came out of great
tribulation, and have washed their robes, and
made them white in the blood of the Lamb."
—Revelation 7:9-14*

These words occur in the well-known vision of
the great multitude in heavenly glory, which no
man could number. In his spirit, the apostle
saw them standing before the throne of God
and of the Lamb, clothed with long white robes,
and with palms in their hands; and they sang
with a loud voice, *"Salvation to our God which
sitteth on the throne, and to the Lamb."* All the
angels answered this song by falling down on

their faces before the throne to worship God and to offer eternal praise and glory to Him.

Then one of the elders, pointing out the great multitude and the clothing which distinguished them put the question to John, *"What are these which are arrayed in white robes, and whence came they?"* John replied, *"Sir, thou knowest."* Then the elder said, *"These are they which came out of great tribulation and have washed their robes, and made them white in the blood of the Lamb. Therefore are they before the throne of God, and serve Him day and night in his temple."*

This explanation, given by one of the elders who stood round the throne, concerning the state of the redeemed in their heavenly glory, is of great value.

It reveals to us the fact that not only in this world of sin and strife is the blood of Jesus the one hope of the sinner, but that in heaven, when every enemy has been subdued, that precious blood will be recognized forever as the ground of our salvation. And we learn that the blood must exercise its power with God in heaven, not only as long as sin has still to be dealt with here beneath, but that through all eternity, each one of the redeemed to the praise and glory of the blood will bear the sign of how the blood has availed for him and that he owes his salvation entirely to it.

If we have a clear insight into this we shall understand better what a true and vital connection there is between *"the sprinkling of the blood"* and the joys of heaven, and that a true intimate connection with the blood on earth will enable the believer while still on earth to share the joy and glory of heaven.

Joy in heaven through the blood is because it is the blood that:

First, bestows the right to a place in heaven;

Second, makes us fit for the pleasures of heaven; and

Last, provides subject matter for the song of heaven.

The Blood Bestows the Right to a Place in Heaven

It is clear that this is the leading thought in the text. In the question, *"What are these which are arrayed in white robes and whence came they?"* the elder desires to awaken attention and inquiry as to who these favored persons really are who stand thus before the throne and before the Lamb, with palms in their hands. And, as he himself gives the reply,

167

we expect that he will surely mention what might be thought to be the most remarkable thing in their appearance. He replies to the question *"Whence came they?"* by saying that *"they come out of great tribulation."* To the question *"Who are these?"* he replies that they have washed their long white robes, and made them white in the blood of the Lamb.

That is the one thing to which, as their distinguishing mark, he draws attention. This alone gives them the right to the place which they occupy in glory. This becomes plainly evident, if we notice the words which immediately follow: *"therefore are they before the throne of God and serve him day and night in his temple; and he that sitteth on the throne shall dwell among them."* *"Therefore,"* it is because of that blood that they are before the throne. They owe it to the blood of the Lamb that they occupy that place so high in glory. The blood gives the right to heaven.

Right to heaven! Can such a thing be spoken of in connection with a condemned sinner? Would it not be better to glory in the mercy of God only, who by free grace admits a sinner to heaven, than to speak of a right to heaven? No! It would not be better: for then we should not understand the value of the blood or why it had to be shed. We should also entertain false conceptions both of our sin and of God's grace, and remain unfit for the full enjoyment of the glorious redemption which the Saviour has accomplished for us.

We have already spoken of *"the casting out of Satan from heaven,"* and have shown from this incident that a holy God acts always according to law. Just as the devil was not *"cast out"* otherwise than according to law and right, so the sinner cannot be admitted in any other way. The prophet said, *"Zion shall be redeemed with judgment and her converts with righteousness"* (Isaiah 1:27). Paul tells us that *"grace reigns through righteousness"* (Romans 5:21). This was the purpose for which God sent His Son into the world. Instead of being afraid that speaking of having a right to enter heaven might belittle grace, it will be seen that the highest glory of grace consists in bestowing that right.

The lack of this insight is sometimes found in the church where it might be least expected. Recently I asked a man who spoke of the hope he had of going to heaven when he died, on what ground he rested his hope. He was not by any means a careless man nor did he trust to his own righteousness, and yet he replied, "Well, I think that I strive my best to seek the Lord, and to do His will." When I told him that this was no ground on which to stand before the judgment seat of a holy God, he appealed to the mercy of God. When I told him again that he needed more than mercy, it appeared to him to be something new to hear that it was the righteousness of God only that could grant him entrance into heaven. It is to be feared that there are many who listen to the preaching of *"justification by faith,"* but who have no idea that they cannot have a share in eternal blessedness save by being declared legally righteous.

Entirely different was the testimony of a certain lad who had not the full use of his intellectual faculties, but whose heart the Spirit of God had enlightened to understand the meaning of the crucifixion of Jesus.

When on his deathbed he was asked about his hope, he intimated that there was a great book, on one of the pages of which his many sins, very many, had been written. Then with the finger of his right hand, he pointed to the palm of his left hand, indicating the print of the nail there. Taking, as it were, something from the pierced hand—he was thinking of the blood that marked it—he showed how all that was written on that page was now blotted out. The blood of the Lamb was the ground of his hope.

The blood of the Lamb gives the believing sinner a right to heaven. *"Behold the Lamb of God which taketh away the sin of the world."* By shedding His blood, He really bore the punishment of sin. He gave Himself up to death really in our place. He gave His life as a ransom for many. Now that the punishment is borne, and our Lord's blood has really been shed as a ransom and appears before the throne of God in heaven, now the righteousness of God declares that, as the sinner's surety had fulfilled all the requirements of the law, both as regards punishment and obedience, God pronounces the sinner who believes in Christ to be righteous. Faith is just the recognition that Christ has really done everything for me, that God's declaration of righteousness is just His declaration that, according to the law and right, I have a title to salvation. God's grace bestows on me the right to heaven. The blood of the Lamb is the evidence of this right. If I have been cleansed by that blood, I can meet death with full confidence: I have a right to heaven.

You desire and hope to get to heaven. Listen then to the answer given to the question: who are they who will find a place before the throne of God? *"They have washed their robes, and made them white in the blood of the Lamb."* That washing takes place, not in heaven and not at death, but here during our life on earth. Do not deceive yourselves by a hope of heaven, if you have not been cleansed, really cleansed, by that precious blood. Do not dare to meet death without knowing that Jesus Himself has cleansed you by His blood.

The Blood Bestows
the Fitness for Heaven

It is of little use for men to have a right to anything unless they are fitted to enjoy it. However costly the gift, it is of little use if the inner disposition necessary to the enjoyment of it is wanting. To bestow the right to heaven on those who are not at the same time prepared for it would give them no pleasure, but would be in conflict with the perfection of all God's works.

The power of the blood of Jesus not only sets open the door of heaven for the sinner but it operates on him in such a divine way that, as he enters heaven, it will appear that the blessedness of heaven and he have been really fitted for each other.

What constitutes the blessedness of heaven, and what the disposition is that is fitted for it, we are told by words connected with our text:

"Therefore are they before the throne of God, and serve him day and night in his temple; and he that sitteth on the throne shall dwell among them. They shall hunger no more, neither thirst any more, neither shall the sun light on them nor any heat; for the Lamb which is in the midst of the throne shall feed

*them, and shall lead them unto living
fountains of water, and God shall wipe
away all tears from their eyes.*
(Revelation 7:15-17)

Nearness to and fellowship with God and
the Lamb constitute the blessedness of heaven.
To be before the throne of God, to see His face,
to serve Him day and night in His temple, to
be overshadowed by Him who sits upon the
throne, to be fed and led by the Lamb—all
these expressions point out how little the
blessedness of heaven depends on anything else
than on God and the Lamb. To see Them, to
have intimacy with Them, to be acknowledged,
loved, and cared for by Them—that is
blessedness.

What preparation is needed for having
such relationship with God and the Lamb? It
consists in two things: inner agreement in
mind and will, and delight in His nearness and
fellowship. Both are purchased by the blood.

Inner Agreement in Mind and Will

There can be no thought of fitness for
heaven apart from oneness with God's will.
How could two dwell together unless they
agreed? And because God is the holy One, the
sinner must be cleansed from his sin and

sanctified, otherwise he remains utterly unfit for what constitutes the happiness of heaven. *"Without holiness no man can see the Lord."* Man's entire nature must be renewed, so that he may think, desire, will, and do what pleases God, not as a matter of mere obedience in keeping a commandment, but from natural pleasure and because he cannot do or will otherwise. Holiness must become his nature.

Is not this just what we have seen that the blood of the Lamb does? *"The blood of Jesus Christ his Son cleanseth us from all sin."* Where reconciliation and pardon are applied by the Holy Spirit and are retained by a living faith, there the blood operates with a divine power, killing sinful lusts and desires. The blood exercises constantly a wonderful cleansing power. In the blood, the power of the death of Jesus operates; we died with Him to sin; through a believing relationship with the blood, the power of the death of Jesus presses into the innermost parts of our hidden life. The blood breaks the power of sin and cleanses from all sin.

The blood sanctifies also. We have seen that cleansing is but one part of salvation, the taking away of sin. The blood does more than this; it takes possession of us for God and inwardly bestows the very same disposition which was in Jesus when He shed His blood. In shedding that blood, He sanctified Himself for us, that we also should be sanctified by the truth. As we delight and lose ourselves in that holy blood, the power of entire surrender to God's will and glory, the power to sacrifice everything and to abide in God's love which inspired the Lord Jesus is efficacious in us.

The blood sanctifies us for the emptying and surrender of ourselves, so that God may take possession of us and fill us with Himself. This is true holiness: to be possessed by and filled with God. This is wrought out by the blood of the Lamb, and so we are prepared here on earth to meet God in heaven with unspeakable joy.

Delight in His Nearness and Fellowship

In addition to having one will with God, we said that fitness for heaven consisted in the desire and capacity for enjoying fellowship with God. In this also, the blood bestows, here on earth, the true preparation for heaven. We have seen how the blood brings us near to God, leading to a priestlike approach. Yes, we have liberty, by the blood, to enter into the Holiest of God's presence, and to make our dwelling place there. We have seen that God attaches to the blood such incomprehensible value that, where the blood is sprinkled, there is His throne of grace. When a heart places itself under the full operation of the blood, there God dwells, and there His salvation is experienced. The blood makes possible the practice of fellowship with God, and not less with the Lamb, the Lord Jesus Himself. Have we forgotten His word, *"He that eateth my flesh and drinketh my blood abideth in me, and I in him"*? The full blessing of the power of the blood, in its highest effect, is full abiding union with Jesus. It is only our unbelief that separates the work from the person, and the blood from the Lord Jesus. It is He, Himself, who cleanses by His blood, who brings us near, and who causes us to drink. It is only through the blood that we are fitted for full fellowship with Jesus in heaven, just as with the Father.

You who are redeemed! Here you can see what is needed to mold you for heaven, to make you, even here, heavenly minded. See that the blood, which always has a place at the throne of grace above, manifests its power always in your hearts. Then your lives will become an unbroken fellowship with God and the Lamb—the foretaste of life in eternal glory. Let the thought enter deeply into your soul: the blood bestows already in the heart, here on earth, the blessedness of heaven. The precious blood makes life on earth and life in heaven one.

The Blood Provides Subject Matter
for the Song of Heaven

What we have hitherto said has been taken
from what the elder stated about the redeemed.
But how far is this their experience and testimony? Have we anything out of their own
mouths concerning this? Yes, they themselves
bear witness. In the song contained in our text,
they were heard to cry with loud voice, *"Salvation to our God which sitteth upon the throne,
and unto the Lamb."* It is as the slain Lamb
that the Lord Jesus is in the midst of the
throne, as a Lamb whose blood had been shed.
As such, He is the object of the worship of the
redeemed.

This appears still more clearly in the new
song that they sing, *"Thou art worthy to take
the book and to open the seals thereof, for thou
hast redeemed us to God by Thy blood, out of
every kindred, and tongue, and nation, and
hast made us unto our God kings and priests"*
(Revelation 5:9-10).

Or in words somewhat different, used by
the apostle in the beginning of the book, where
he, under the impression of all that he had
seen and heard in heaven concerning the place
which the Lamb occupied, at the first mention
of the name of the Lord Jesus, cried out, *"Unto
him that loved us and washed us from our sins
in His own blood, and hath made us kings and*

priests unto God and his Father; to him be glory and dominion for ever, Amen." (Revelation 1:5-6).

Without ceasing, the blood of the Lamb continues to be the power to awaken the saved to their song of joy and thanksgiving because, in the death of the cross, the sacrifice took place in which He gave Himself for them and won them for Himself. Because the blood is the eternal seal of what He did and of the love which moved Him to do it, it remains also the inexhaustible, overflowing fountain of heavenly bliss.

That we may the better understand this, notice the expression: *"Him that loved us and washed us from our sins in His own blood."* In all our consideration about the blood of Jesus, we have had till now no occasion intentionally to stop there. And of all the glorious things which the blood means, this is one of the most glorious: His blood is the sign, the measure, yes, the impartation of His love. Each application of His blood, each time that He causes the soul to experience its power, is a fresh out-flowing of His wonderful love. The full experience of the power of the blood in eternity will be nothing else than the full revelation of how He gave Himself up for us, and how He gives Himself to us in a love eternal, unending, as incomprehensible as God Himself.

"Him who loved us and washed us from our sins in his own blood." This love is indeed incomprehensible. What has not that love moved Him to do? He gave Himself for us; He became sin for us; He was made a curse for us. Who would dare to use such language; who could ever have dared to think such a thing if God had not revealed it to us by His Spirit? That He really gave Himself up for us, not because it was laid upon Him to do so, but by the impulse of a love that really longed for us, that we might for ever be identified with Him.

Because it is such a divine wonder, we feel it so little. But, blessed be the Lord! there is a time coming when we shall feel it, when under the ceaseless and immediate love-sharing of the heavenly life, we shall be filled and satisfied with that love. Yes, praised be the Lord! Even here on earth there is hope that through a better knowledge of and a more perfect trust in the blood, the Spirit will more powerfully shed abroad *"the love of God in our hearts."* There is nothing to prevent our hearts being filled with the love of the Lamb and our mouths with His praise here on earth by faith, as is done in heaven by sight. Each experience of the power of the blood will become increasingly an experience of the love of Jesus.

It has been said that it is not desirable to lay too much emphasis on the word *blood,* that it sounds coarse, and the thought expressed by it can be conveyed in a way more in accordance with our modern habit of speaking or thinking. I must acknowledge that I do not share in this view. I receive that word as coming, not just from John, but from the Lord Himself. I am deeply convinced that the word chosen by the Spirit of God, and by Him made living and filled with the power of that eternal life whence the song containing it comes to us, carries in itself a power of blessing surpassing our understanding. Changing the expression into our way of thinking has all the imperfection of a human translation. He who desires to know and experience *what the Spirit says unto the churches* will accept the word by faith, as having come from heaven, as the word in which the joy and power of eternal life is enfolded in a most peculiar manner. Those expressions, *Thy blood* and *the blood of the Lamb,* will make the Holiest, the place of God's glory, resound eternally with the joyful notes of *the new song.*

Heavenly joy through the blood of the Lamb will be the portion of all, here on earth, who with undivided heart yield to its power; and of all above, in heaven, who have become worthy to take a place among the multitude around the throne.

My comrades in redemption, we have learned what those in heaven say and how they sing about the blood. Let us pray earnestly that these tidings may have the effect on us which our Lord intended. We have seen that to live a real heavenly life, it is necessary to abide in the full power of blood. The blood bestows the right to enter heaven.

As the blood of reconciliation, it works out in the soul the full, living consciousness which belongs to those who are at home in heaven. It brings us really into the Holiest, near to God. It makes us fit for heaven.

As the cleansing blood, it delivers from the lust and power of sin, and preserves us in the fellowship of the light and life of the Holy God. The blood inspires the song of praise in heaven. As the blood of the Lamb *"who loved us and gave himself for us,"* it speaks not only of what He has done us, but chiefly of Him who has done all. In the blood, we have the most perfect impartation of Himself. He who by faith gives himself up to experience to the full, what the blood is able do, will soon find an entrance into a life of happy singing of praise and love, that only heaven itself can surpass.

My comrades in redemption! This life is for you and me. May the blood be all our glory, not only at the cross with its awful wonders, but also at the throne. Let us plunge deep, and ever deeper, into the living fountain of blood of the Lamb. Let us open our hearts wide, and ever wider, for its operation. Let us firmly, and ever more firmly, believe in the ceaseless cleansing by which the great Eternal Priest Himself will apply that blood to us. Let us pray with burning desire, and ever more desire, that nothing—yes, nothing—may be in our hearts that does not experience the power of the blood. Let us unite joyfully, and ever more joyfully, in the song of the great multitude, who know of nothing so glorious this: *"Thou hast redeemed us to God, by thy blood."*

May our life on earth become what it ought to be: one ceaseless song to *"Him who loved and washed us from our sins in his own blood, and hath made us kings and priests unto God and his Father."*

"To him be the glory and dominion for ever and ever." Amen.